FINDING CONFIDENCE IN CONFLICT

How to Negotiate Anything and Live Your Best Life

Kwame Christian, M.A., Esq.
Director of the American Negotiation Institute

To the fans of the TEDx and the podcast, thank you for your continued support and for being the motivation and inspiration for my best work.

To my staff, interns, family and friends, thank you for your continuous encouragement. This is as much your win as it is mine.

To those of you who are new to my content, welcome! Thank you for reading and please connect with me online (LinkedIn and Instagram are my favorites).

Kwame

This book gives you a great foundation for having these difficult conversations but there's much more to learn and we can help you every step of the way.

Online Course: Negotiate Anything: Finding Confidence in Conflict.

Visit our website: Gain access to our robust online program that will give you the confidence you need to succeed and the most powerful persuasive techniques. Visit www.AmericanNegotiationInstitute.com/Course and use the word **"confidence"** for a 10% discount.

Custom Workshops and Training: We work with organizations just like yours to create custom trainings. Visit our website to see how we can help.

Coaching: We also provide 1 on 1 coaching for professionals looking to get an edge or overcome their personal barriers for success.

Negotiate Anything Podcast: This is the #1 negotiation podcast in the world. We have leading experts on the show every week to share their best tips.

Ask With Confidence Podcast: This podcast is all about women in negotiation. Our host, Katherine Knapke, has incredible women leaders on the show to explore how to be successful in negotiation.

TABLE OF CONTENTS

WHO AM I?

My parents immigrated from the Caribbean to further their education. They met at Howard University in Washington, D.C. My dad became a surgeon and my mom earned her PhD and became a professor.

A job opportunity opened up for my dad after residency in a small, rural town in Ohio named Tiffin. We looked different, we sounded different, and I often found it difficult to fit in. One day in particular left an indelible mark on my psyche.

It was a brisk autumn day and the sun shone brightly on the pavement at the playground. I was in first grade and it was recess. I remember happily going outside and looking for some friends to play with.

I went up to one group of kids and asked if I could play with them and they said no. Then I went to another group of kids who were playing kickball and asked if I could play with them and they said no. I got so desperate that I even tried to play with the girls. They didn't want to play with me, either. I spent the entire recess looking for friends, but nobody wanted to play with me.

Eventually, the bell rang and everybody ran inside. As soon as I got inside, I started bawling. No matter how much I tried, I couldn't pull myself together. To this day I've never felt more alone and embarrassed. When the teacher saw me, she hugged me and tried her best to console me.

At that moment, I vowed to myself that this would never, ever, ever happen again. No matter what it took, I was going to have friends and people were going to like me. I was never going to feel so alone again.

After that day, I went out of my way to be friendly and nice to everyone. As the years went by, I became more well-liked and eventually became one of the most popular kids in school.

However, this came with a price. I became deathly terrified of conflict because I didn't want to risk losing the friends I had worked so hard to get. I became a people-pleaser, a pushover. It felt impossible to stand up for myself. This led me to agree when I disagreed and avoid confrontation at all costs.

Our greatest weaknesses often lie in the shadows of our greatest strengths. Although I was gregarious, fun-loving, successful and popular, I was completely lacking in confidence when it came to critical conversations in my life. I felt impotent and weak and I hated myself for it.

All this changed when my mentor told me something I'll never forget. He said, "Kwame, there's a difference between being liked and being respected. If you want to have personal and professional success, you need to be willing to engage with conflict."

I had goals. I was ambitious. I wanted to help people and I wanted to have a large-scale impact. My mentor made it abundantly clear that it would be impossible for me to accomplish a fraction of what I had in mind if I couldn't overcome this fear.

People look at me today and see a confident man who travels the country teaching professionals how to negotiate effectively and manage conflict. They see a man who willingly and eagerly thrusts himself into the middle of conflicts as a mediator and into high-level negotiations as a lawyer. They see my current confidence and they assume it comes naturally.

I wasn't born this way; I was built this way. In this book, I share the tools and strategies that I used to find confidence in conflict. You'll learn how to pinpoint the genesis of your performance gap, the modern psychological tools you can use to close the gap and build confidence, the secrets to developing an empowering mindset, and a powerful technique called compassionate curiosity that you can use in your most difficult conflicts and negotiations. Reading this book is the first step on your lifelong journey toward self-confidence and mastery in the realm of difficult conversations.

INTRODUCTION

Throughout this book, I'll be talking about negotiation, conflict, and difficult conversations, so it is important to first define them.

<u>Negotiation</u>: any conversation where someone in the conversation wants something.

<u>Conflict</u>: a negotiation with attitude.

<u>Difficult conversation</u>: any negotiation or conflict.

As the Director of the American Negotiation Institute, I initially wanted to write a book that got into the nitty-gritty of negotiation theory and addressed the biggest concerns of professionals in the realm of negotiation and conflict management. Hosting the top-ranked negotiation podcast in the world, *Negotiate Anything*, with over 1.5 million downloads and listeners in 181 different countries provided me with a unique opportunity to hear these concerns directly from my listeners. So I asked them what prevented them from growing in their negotiation skills.

I learned something fascinating. Their biggest barrier in difficult conversations wasn't strategic or tactical; it was something deeper. Here's what I learned:

1. People avoid or struggle in difficult conversations because they feel fear and anxiety.

2. People don't know what to say in the midst of difficult conversations.

We've been giving recipes to people who are afraid to get in the kitchen. Their issues were psychological and emotional. This made sense when I thought back on my own life. I was able to overcome this through my love of psychology and my desire to use my passion to overcome my fears.

My model for overcoming fear and finding confidence in conflict is rooted in cognitive behavioral therapy (CBT). CBT is a form of therapy that is scientifically proven to be effective for a number of psychological problems, including phobias and anxiety.[1]

CBT is rooted in the belief that psychological problems are based, in part, on unhelpful ways of thinking and on learned patterns of unhelpful behavior. Thus, CBT typically involves a combination of treatments geared toward changing your patterns of thought and patterns of behavior.

According to the American Psychological Association, typical treatments regarding thought patterns include the following:

1. Developing a greater sense of confidence in one's abilities.

2. Learning to recognize one's distortions in thinking that are creating problems, and then to reevaluate them in light of reality.

3. Using problem-solving skills to cope with difficult situations.[2]

My approach to helping you to find confidence in conflict is modeled after this proven methodology. As such, when we utilize the approaches from CBT and apply them to our everyday lives, we can reap the benefits from decades of psychological research.

As such, my goals for this book are as follows:

1. Help you to gain a better understanding of the psychology behind the fear and anxiety underlying difficult conversations.

2. Help you to identify your own unique psychological barriers in difficult conversations and provide you with a new, action-oriented mindset.

3. Provide you with a simple framework you can use to increase your confidence in difficult conversations.

This revolutionary approach underlies all of the negotiation and conflict management seminars I conduct when I travel the country and consult with companies. Every tool, tactic, and strategy is borne from the firm foundations of cognitive psychology and neuroscience. The difference is that I focus first on *your* psychology by exploring the emotions, fears, and anxiety you experience as a negotiator.

Once that has been addressed, we focus on the psychology of the other party.

Choosing to improve this skill may be one of the most important decisions you ever make, because the best things in life often lie on the other side of a difficult conversation. You will fail to enjoy the best versions of your personal and professional lives if you are unable or unwilling to engage in difficult conversations. My goal is to empower you to change your life by changing the way you approach difficult conversations.

About the Book/Book Structure

The goal of this book is to provide you with a single technique you can use both internally and externally called Compassionate Curiosity. You can use this technique to win the internal negotiation with yourself and the external negotiation with others. You'll also learn how to recognize the breakdowns in communications that make conflicts hostile, awkward, and unproductive and how to get things back on track.

The Compassionate Curiosity Framework is comprised of the following three steps:

1. Acknowledge Emotions

2. Get Curious with Compassion

3. Joint Problem-Solving

The Compassionate Curiosity Framework provides you with a clear framework for approaching *all* difficult conversations, from the boardroom to the kitchen table. The benefit of a framework is that it provides you with clarity and direction as you prepare for and ultimately navigate your most difficult conversations. Structure helps to reduce stress and anxiety while minimizing your cognitive load. In other words, you'll be more confident and less inhibited.

The Compassionate Curiosity Framework not only helps you to win your external negotiations, but also your internal negotiations. You can use the exact same steps as a tool of self reflection to help you to gain clarity and overcome emotional hurdles.

I believe that conversations are inherently complex, but they don't need to be complicated. What's the difference?

- If something is complicated, it is difficult to execute, analyze, understand, or explain.[3]

- When something is complex, it is "composed of many interconnected parts."[4]

This framework will simplify these interactions, help you to resolve and manage conflict, and deal with difficult conversations and difficult people. It will also help you to avoid the critical mistakes that destroy relationships and your chances for success.

The Compassionate Curiosity Framework came from a mental exercise. I looked back on my experience serving as a mediator in well over 100 mediations and my years as an attorney negotiating in the business world. I asked myself, if I were to articulate my universal approach to these difficult conversations in the simplest fashion, how would I do that?

One of the biggest benefits of having a framework is that it helps you to understand what is important and what is unimportant. A predictable structure allows you to limit your options, so you are not thrown off course by unnecessary externalities. This allows you to direct your focused attention on what matters, while ignoring what doesn't matter. Cognitive energy is precious; your attention is precious. We want to allocate these precious resources in the most efficient manner possible.

The paradox of choice holds that the more options that become available, the less likely you are to make a selection. I bring this up because there are hundreds of great persuasion techniques. However, I've learned that the majority of people won't use them because the sheer magnitude of choices is both overwhelming and paralyzing. Because of that, I'm not going to inundate you with a laundry list of techniques and strategies.

This book is about taking action. By limiting the focus to a single technique, there is less mental overwhelm, which increases the likelihood of action and successful execution. I also encourage you to customize Compassionate Curiosity to fit your authentic negotiation style. You can take this and make it your own.

To highlight the lessons from the book, I will share stories from my mediations, my negotiations as an attorney, and, most importantly, my experience as a father. My most challenging negotiations are with my two-year-old son, Kai. I enjoy sharing these stories because, in many ways, the same psychological principles are at play in difficult conversations with adults. To see cute pictures of Kai, check out my Instagram: Kwame_Christian.

I became more successful in the business and legal world when I recognized that, in many cases, I was really negotiating with the person's inner toddler. I wasn't going to meet my needs if I couldn't *first* speak to their underlying emotional needs.

Lastly, we've created a free workbook you can use to maximize the impact of these valuable lessons. It will help you to customize the content and includes our most popular negotiation guides — the business negotiation guide, the conflict management guide, and the salary negotiation guide. You can download your free workbook online at www.AmericanNegotiationInstitute.com/workbook.

Working from the Inside Out

One of the problems you face in difficult conversations is that you work from the outside in. You see your barrier to success as something that lives outside of yourself. It's either the other person, the circumstances, or your lack of knowledge or experience in difficult conversations that you assume is causing the issue.

The problem with this is that it is more likely that your biggest barrier to success lies within the confines of your own mind. As a result, your unaddressed internal struggle manifests itself in an inability to engage effectively in difficult conversations, if you engage them at all. Your issue isn't tactical; it's psychological.

Once you realize it's internal, you can work to solve the problem. If you continue convincing yourself that it's external, you'll keep blaming things other than yourself and never take full responsibility for these outcomes. Or you'll search for a solution for the wrong problem. You'll keep strategizing and learning techniques when that alone won't help. You need to look inside.

I remember one client reporting back to me in tears because, despite the strategy and tactics we discussed, she failed to stand up for herself and negotiate her salary. Between tears she said, "I just feel so stupid. I don't know why I can't do this."

It's not stupidity you feel; it's cognitive dissonance. You know what you want, you know what you need to do, but when the time is right you do something else. You betray yourself and it hurts.

What makes this even more frustrating is that you don't understand why. Humans are meaning-making machines. We constantly seek understanding and meaning in all aspects of our lives and when we can't understand something, it is especially frustrating. Also, when there is a mystery, we tend to focus on that thing obsessively. As a result, we obsessively focus on what we can't understand and that makes us even more frustrated.

This book is for Ashley, an accomplished professional who has no problem advocating on behalf of her children and her company, but struggles to advocate for herself. She excels when she defends the interests of others but can't seem to defend herself.

This book is for Michael, a manager who is struggling to persuade and influence his team because of his inability to connect with his own emotions and the emotions of others.

This book is for Jon, an entrepreneur who knows exactly what he needs to get out of his business deals and knows what strategy to implement but, despite this knowledge, finds himself unable to execute or avoiding the necessary conversations. If he does muster up the strength to engage in conversations, his arguments come out so tepidly that not even he is convinced. He is overwhelmed with anxiety and fear.

This book is for Jessica, who struggles to convince others of her worth because she is not yet convinced of her own worth. She works hard and gets results, but struggles to get the recognition she deserves. Not only is she trying to negotiate for more money, but more recognition. However, she is too timid to speak up and let people truly know the extent of her contribution.

Parenting isn't about being perfect all the time; it's about being good enough most of the time. Similarly, my goal isn't for you to become a perfect negotiator, because that's an unrealistic goal that fosters an unhealthy mindset. Instead, I want you to build the confidence and adopt the mindset necessary to consistently put yourself in the best position for success.

Chapter 1

WHY IS THIS SO HARD?

These thoughts and feelings are often little more than evidence of a healthy, functioning mind.

There's a joke in psychology that says people study or do research on the problems that they or a loved one have. For example, if a psychologist has struggled with depression, they will like study depression. If your family has a history of Alzheimer's, you are likely to study Alzheimer's. For me, my interest in psychology developed because I had a lot of fear and anxiety when it came to difficult conversations and certain social interactions. I wanted to learn more about the human mind so I could help myself and help others as a clinical psychologist. That was my goal.

Somewhere along the way, my impressionable mind was bitten by the political bug and I changed course to study law and public policy. In many ways, what I do now reorients me back to my love of psychology and my desire to help people live their best lives by overcoming their fears and anxieties.

One of the things I loved about psychology was the fact that it helped me feel normal. I didn't feel broken or defective when I learned about how the brain works. I found that these fears and anxieties are, in most cases, simply the manifestation of a healthy, functioning mind.

The goal in this chapter is to normalize the human experience. These inhibiting emotional responses are hard enough to deal with, but become even harder when you feel as though you're abnormal or like you're broken. The reality is much less damning: you're human. You'll be able to overcome the fear, anxiety, and self-doubt much faster when you're able to accept your humanity and create strategies to work around it.

The solutions provided in this book come from decades of research in neuroscience and cognitive psychology. Considering what we know about neuroplasticity, in order for these strategies to work, they need to be implemented with rigorous consistency. Don't think of them so much as strategies to achieve a specific outcome; think of them more as opportunities to engage in mental training. Will these exercises help you in the short term? Yes. However, that is simply an incidental byproduct. Short-term benefits are great, but what I want for you is lasting, lifelong change. It's important to focus on the long term versus the short term because the outcomes in these difficult conversations are not like math, where predictable input leads to predictable output. You could do everything right strategically, tactically, and socially, and still not end up with the desired outcome. I don't want this to be unduly disappointing because failures are part of the process.

Having a deeper understanding of psychology will help you to be more creative in difficult conversations because you'll have an appreciation of what is going on beneath the surface. You will know what the psychological barrier is and you'll have an idea of how to get there. The puzzle is trying to figure out what you need to do or say in order to create the right state of mind for persuasion.

A lot of times, negotiation experts say that you should think of these as normal conversations in which there is nothing to fear. That's true. However, we know the issue isn't logical; it's emotional.

Outlining the logical and rational reasons as to why people shouldn't be afraid is ultimately unhelpful. Negotiation is scary. Conflict is scary. The more we try to tell ourselves it's not, the less likely we will be able to overcome the fear and operate in spite of it.

After reading this chapter, you'll learn that you have more control over your thoughts and emotions than you originally imagined. This is empowering and it is backed by research. However, this also means that we need to accept a greater level of responsibility for our performance in these difficult conversations. It is not automatic yet, but if we don't take the time and push through right now, it will be harder to do so tomorrow.

The Brain: What's Going on in There?

Let's start off by introducing the most important brain structures and concepts that relate to difficult conversations.

The Amygdala and Limbic System

The amygdala is part of the limbic system, which is one of the most primitive brain structures, and it is known as the lizard brain. It is the creator of our emotions, both pleasant and unpleasant. However, since unpleasant things can kill you faster than pleasant things, it is much more sensitive to the negative.

It produces quick, primal responses to *perceived* threats that were once critical to keeping us alive, way back in the day when death lurked around every corner. The problem is that society has evolved faster than our brains. As a result, we struggle in conflict today because we are fighting modern-day battles with prehistoric tools.

Have you ever said something in the heat of the moment that you immediately knew was a mistake? This is called an amygdala hijack and it takes you from rational to irrational in the blink of an eye.

These quick, emotional responses are rooted in fear. We have three responses to fear: fight, flight, and the often-overlooked freeze, which is also known as the deer-in-headlights response.

Evolutionarily speaking, the limbic system was one of the first brain structures to form. The frontal lobe and pre-frontal cortex, both of which are involved with higher level thinking and emotional regulation, evolved later. This suggests that our natural state is emotional and explains why becoming emotional is easy and rational thinking takes more effort.

You will interpret situations emotionally before you interpret them rationally, so it is critical to slow down and take your time in the midst of conflict. You need to give yourself time to shift from your automatic response to your reasoned response.[5]

Unsurprisingly, none of these automatic fear responses lead to favorable outcomes in our difficult conversations. There are predictable ramifications for these responses:

- Fighting leads you to destroy relationships.

- Fleeing leads you to run from opportunities to improve relationships.

- Freezing leads you to exist in a false relationship.

Your preferred fear response will be a product of your lived experience. Looking back at the story about how nobody would play with me, we can see that my fear of losing friends as a result of difficult conversations caused me to either freeze or flee. I would actively avoid the difficult conversations or become a doormat and let others walk all over me. When you understand these automatic, instinctual responses to difficult conversations it's easy to appreciate why we can't rely on simply doing what feels right or safe in the moment.

We need to learn to be more aware of these impulses because our natural responses in these situations will let us down. The Compassionate Curiosity framework is an *unnatural* response to difficult conversations. We're replacing our instincts with thoughtfulness. This increased awareness will lead to increased control and more favorable outcomes in these difficult conversations. This model works because it is informed by cognitive psychology and recruits the usage of our most evolved brain structure, the prefrontal cortex.

The Prefrontal Cortex

There was a railroad foreman in the 1800s named Phineas Gage. Gage is famous in psychological lore because of his unfortunate contribution to neuroscience.

Gage was the victim of a freak accident where an iron rod passed cleanly through the front of his head, destroying much of his frontal lobe and prefrontal cortex. Before the accident, Gage was responsible, well-mannered, and dependable. After the accident, he became an unstable alcoholic who struggled to retain a job.

The prefrontal cortex is the home of the executive functions. This is where you'll find some of the brain's highest-level cognitive processes. These functions allow you to consider options and ideas, be creative, and engage in problem-solving. They also allow you to focus, resist temptations (self-control), think before acting, and regulate your emotions.[6] Researchers are discovering that the development of the executive functions is one of the most critical elements of academic and professional success.

The prefrontal cortex is the most important part of the brain when it comes to your performance in difficult conversations. The beauty of Compassionate Curiosity is that it allows you to engage your prefrontal cortex more consistently when the heat is on. It has the added benefit of allowing you to structure and approach difficult conversations in a way that also engages the prefrontal cortex of the other party.

There is no point in saying something if the recipient isn't in a mental state that is capable of receiving it. With Compassionate Curiosity, you walk the other party from emotionality to rationality and put yourself in the best position for success.

Have you ever had that feeling where you don't know what to say in the middle of a difficult conversation? Why does it seem like we can't think clearly when it matters most? This occurs because stress inhibits our ability to engage in higher-level thinking.

Our body's stress response system is known as the hypothalamic pituitary adrenal (HPA) axis and follows this pattern:

1. The amygdala perceives a threat and activates your body's stress response by sending an alert signal to your hypothalamus.[7]

2. The hypothalamus then tells your adrenal glands to produce adrenaline.

3. The adrenaline increases your heart rate and causes your heart rate to elevate as it rushes blood to your muscles to respond to the threat, which increases your blood pressure. It also causes you to breathe faster to send more oxygen to your brain and increase alertness.

The stress response is germane to this discussion because the prefrontal cortex is "the brain region that is most sensitive to the detrimental effects of stress exposure. Even quite mild acute uncontrollable stress can cause a rapid and dramatic loss of prefrontal cognitive abilities."[8] Thus, when it matters most, our brains are functioning at a less than optimal level. This ex- plains why we come up with the best comebacks hours later in the shower. The intense emotional state has subsided and now that you're relaxed you're able to think at a higher level.

This is why role playing is such a critical part of my negotiation workshops. The more experience you have in these scenarios, the less stress you will feel and the clearer your mind will be when you encounter these situations in your own life. You can use vivid visualization in lieu of this training to achieve a similar result. Visualization has played such a significant role in sports psychology for this very reason.

Familiarizing yourself with the situation before the difficult conversation through thorough preparation is another way to reduce your stress levels during the conversation. Competence breeds confidence. The more you know, the better you'll feel.

In your free workbook, you'll find a free negotiation preparation guide for business negotiations, salary negotiations, and conflict management. To get your workbook, go to www.AmericanNegotiationInstitute.com/workbook.

Because of the deleterious impact of stress on the prefrontal cortex, the Compassionate Curiosity Framework is intentionally simple. I want you to be able to remember exactly what to do and how to do it despite the heat of these difficult conversations. It's often unrealistic to expect ourselves to recall and then successfully implement more complex strategies in the midst of difficult conversations.

This deeper understanding of the key brain structures at play during these difficult conversations helps to understand why I share stories of my "hostile" negotiations with my two-year-old, Kai, even though I have hundreds of stories from practicing law and serving as a mediator. Children struggle to control their active amygdalae until their prefrontal cortex develops and the executive functions can take hold. The prefrontal cortex doesn't fully develop until the early to mid-20s.[9] The active amygdala is still there in adulthood, but it's better controlled.

In the first step of the Compassionate Curiosity framework, we're talking to their inner toddler—the emotional part of their brain. We must first calm the amygdala before we can speak to the prefrontal cortex.

If you don't know exactly what to say or which tactic to use, knowledge of psychology allows you to make an educated guess as to their current mental and emotional state. From there, we can conduct the conversation in a way that leads them to a mental state that is more conducive to connection, understanding, and negotiation.

Are We Capable of Change?

The brain is a remarkable organ that is capable of significant change. We can shape our mind by restructuring the neural connections inside of our brains through a process called neuroplasticity.

"Mental activity is not only the product of the brain but also a shaper of it."[10] This means that by consciously and consistently controlling our patterns and thoughts, we can change our brain on the neural level.

Habits are a great example of neuroplasticity in action. Habits come about as the result of a trigger, an action, and a reward. The brain creates a neural connection between these three steps that is reinforced through repetition. That's why people, for example, put their pants on starting with the same leg every time. When you look beneath the surface, what you'll see is that the consistent implementation of certain behaviors in response to certain triggers actually changes our brain structures.

This is why becoming more aware of your emotions is a critical part of this process. Your emotions are tied to some kind of impulse to act. They make you want to do something. Even if you are paralyzed with fear, not taking action is a form of action.

The Compassionate Curiosity Framework uses our emotions as a trigger as we create a new habit of engagement in difficult conversations.

What is your natural response if a fuzzy sphere weighing 58.5 grams is hurling toward you at 120 miles per hour? Your amygdala registers a threat to your safety, elevates your heart rate and fill your muscles with blood in order for you to leap out of the way to safety. However, if you are a professional tennis player, your *natural* response is to focus on the ball, turn your hips, pull your racquet back, step *toward* the ball, swing the racquet forward, and make contact. What's the difference? Professional tennis players have been able to create new neural connections and thus change the structure of their brains over the course of years of training and consistent repetition. They intentionally built their brain to respond in this "unnatural" way.

We, too, can change our brains through diligent practice and repetition. This is another reason why I include role-playing scenarios in my workshops. I see it as an opportunity to solidify the patterns of thought and behavior that lead to favorable outcomes in negotiation. Similarly, this is why we need to be intentional about taking every possible opportunity we have to practice these skills. The Compassionate Curiosity Framework can be implemented at home and at work, so there are ample opportunities to flex your new cognitive muscles. Every time you do, you are making changes to your brain that will lead to improved performance and less stress during your future conflicts.

We change our brains with every thought, decision, and action. That's why it's critical to be mindful of our thought and behavior patterns. Every social interaction is an opportunity to engage in this mental exercise. The time for change is now and the choice for change is yours.

Chapter 2

Understanding Our Emotional Barriers: Fear and Anxiety

It doesn't matter if you have the keys to persuasion and conflict resolution if you are too afraid to unlock the door.

People often ask me, "How do you eliminate emotions from these difficult conversations?" The answer is simple: (1) you can't eliminate emotion from these conversations, and (2) you wouldn't want to eliminate emotions from the equation, even if you could. The second part of my response catches people off guard because we typically see emotions as a negative thing. For example, the word "emotional" is more likely to be used as an insult than a compliment, especially in the business world.

The reality is that emotions play a significant role in the decision-making process. When persuading, we can't simply focus on how the other side *thinks* about the situation;

we need to also consider how they *feel* about the situation. Therefore, the goal isn't to eliminate your emotions or the emotions of others; the goal is to manage the respective emotional states to put yourself in the best position for success.

The first step in Compassionate Curiosity is acknowledging emotions. This is because naming our emotions gives us power over them.[11] We feel bad when we experience negative emotions. If that's not bad enough, the negativity is compounded by the fact that we don't feel like we should be feeling this way (especially in the business world). As a result, not only do we feel bad, but we also feel bad about feeling bad, which makes things worse. With Compassionate Curiosity, we look at emotions, both ours and the other party's, in a nonjudgmental fashion guided by genuine curiosity.

Negative emotions play an important role in alerting us to potential threats. Don't treat the products of your emotional alert system as absolute truth; think of them as a signal to investigate. Once we receive that signal, we can use it as a trigger to activate our new habit of engagement by using the Compassionate Curiosity Framework.

Managing your emotions isn't about turning yourself into an unfeeling automaton, it's about recognizing these thoughts as what they are, thoughts. They're not truths; they are thoughts. We need to accept them as such.

When we see a positive thought, we need to label it as a thought, and when we see the benefit of that thought we can then intentionally choose to engage with it. On the other hand, when we have a negative thought, we need to label it as a thought, and then intentionally decide not to engage with it.

With negative thoughts, it's not about resisting; it's about letting go. We need to shift from thinking about managing our emotions in terms of willpower and control to thinking about it in terms of awareness. What is happening in your mind? Are these thoughts helpful or hurtful? Then make the decision to engage with the thoughts that help you and let go of the thoughts that hurt you.

The two emotions we'll focus on for the purpose of this book are fear and anxiety.

Fear

When it comes to understanding some of the most inexplicable aspects of human psychology, it is helpful to look at them through an evolutionary lens.

Early humans were nomadic and moved in small groups or tribes. They depended on each other for everything: food, shelter, support, and survival. Staying in a group wasn't a choice; it was a necessity. If you were separated from your group, what happened to you? You would almost certainly die. Thus, in the early days of humanity, rejection equaled death.

Now let's fast forward to today. In today's society, if we wanted to, we could live a life of relative isolation. We have advanced to a point where we can design a life where we can depend almost entirely on ourselves. However, despite the fact that the immediate threat of death is not associated with rejection, we still feel that painful and scary pang of rejection in business and social settings where we need to ask for what we want. It triggers the same kind of fear that we would've felt tens of thousands of years ago.

Our amygdala doesn't distinguish between real and imagined threats, nor does it significantly distinguish between physical and emotional threats. Thus, our stress response system responds in largely the same way to *every* perceived threat.

This response makes us feel uncomfortable, it makes us feel anxious, and it makes us feel exposed. The reason we don't engage in difficult conversations isn't because we don't have a strong enough drive to achieve the positive outcomes that are in question, nor is it because we don't know what to do or say. The main reason why we don't engage in difficult conversations is because we don't want to risk feeling that momentary discomfort of rejection, even though difficult conversations provide us with the perfect opportunity to get *exactly* what we want and need.

The fear of isolation and rejection can manifest itself in a myriad of ways. As it relates to difficult conversations, most critical manifestations of this fear can be seen in the fear of failure, threats to your ego, imposter syndrome, the fear of awkwardness, and discomfort with a perceived lack of control.

Fear of Failure

Fear of failure is the number one cause of negotiaphobia.[12] This fear can be utterly paralyzing; it prevents us from taking action. We know what we want and we know in general what we need to do in order to get what we want (ask for it!), and yet we don't do it.

What's ironic about this is that inaction as a result of the fear of failure guarantees that which we fear the most. We don't seek out difficult conversations because things are perfect and we have everything we want. We engage in difficult conversations because we want to make things better and improve our situation. Hope-based strategies that are rooted in inaction cede the control of our fate to others. As Martin Luther King Jr. said, "progress never rolls in on wheels of inevitability."[13] Committed action is required.

Threats to Your Personal Identity

We are two imperfect people sharing our versions of the truth.

Another reason why failure is seen as so threatening is the fact that we wrap our identities up in the need to be right to the point where we are unable to distinguish between the value of the point in question and our value as a person. Failure then becomes a threat to our self-worth.

This threat to our identity results in us failing to engage in these conversations in a meaningful way because we don't want to risk our self-worth. Essentially, we're saying to ourselves, "who am I if I'm not right?"

We look at being wrong like it is some kind of disease and the only way that we can protect ourselves is by infecting others with the disease before they infect us. Being wrong isn't a problem, but vilifying someone for being wrong is. You should look at being wrong no differently than a doctor looks at disease. Once a malady is identified, the doctor seeks to heal. We "heal" each other in these difficult conversations by remedying misunderstandings and ignorance. This is done by sharing information and listening. Disease doesn't denigrate us and neither should being wrong.

Needless to say, it is highly problematic to conflate who you are as a person and what you achieve in negotiation. Have any of you tried to negotiate with a two-year-old? As a father, I can tell you that my self-worth would be destroyed if I based it on my ability to persuade Kai. The fact of the matter is that our ability to impact the outcome and change someone's perspective is limited because we are not the only part of the equation. Agreement requires mutual assent. Although we have the ability to persuade and influence others' perspectives, this ability is limited.

The simple solution is to replace the emotional need to be right with a genuine desire to learn. We need to approach these conversations with a spirit of curiosity that allows us to explore the situation and work with the other party to find a mutually agreeable solution. We're shifting our focus from the outcome and "winning" to the process itself. Let your curiosity guide you through the conversation.

The interesting thing is that being mindful of the process and being led by curiosity will ultimately result in more favorable outcomes. However, it requires humility to approach conversations in this way. As you start to do this, you will realize that you feel significantly less pressure as you engage in these difficult conversations because your goal is to learn, not defend your honor and self-worth. The other party will be more receptive of your points because they sense that you're listening and interested in hearing their perspective, which makes it more likely for them to reciprocate and listen to you. The reality is that, at best, we're just two imperfect people sharing our versions of the truth.

Imposter Syndrome

"Self-worth must come before self-defense. You can't defend something if you are not convinced of its value."[14]

Our self-esteem comes entirely from our thoughts and perceptions. Therefore, although reality may change, our self-esteem may stay the same and vice versa.

Everyone has an internal voice and, unfortunately, this internal voice has a habit of being negative and critical. It knows exactly what to say to bring us down and crush our self-esteem. It reminds us of who we used to be, what we've done in the past, and why we can't succeed. No matter what you achieve or how mature you are, this voice never goes away. Your only option is to learn to live with it. When the inner voice criticizes you, it might not be true, but it is certainly compelling.[15]

What's interesting is that this negative and critical internal voice is a protective psychological mechanism. Every opportunity to advance comes with a risk. The internal voice only sees the possible negative outcomes and constantly reminds you of them. This results in you staying nestled safely within your comfort zone. This is akin to the fear of success. Even though we are provided with opportunities for success and advancement, attaining them requires you to step outside of your comfort zone, which is distressing even if it is for a good reason.

That negative voice that tells you not to engage is there to serve one purpose—it is not meant to help you advance, it's not meant to improve your life or to excel, *it's meant to protect what you have.* Think of it like a well-intentioned but over-protective parent. "Don't climb that tree; you might get hurt." "Don't run so fast; you might fall down." "Don't go outside; there are scary people out there." The goal is to keep you nestled safely within your comfort zone.

The reality is the comfort zone only *feels* safe, which doesn't necessarily mean that it *is* safe. Psychologically speaking, it's easy to mistake what is familiar with what is safe. Those are two different things. What's really happening is that before we can ask for what we want, or stand up for ourselves in order to try to get what we want, we try to avoid rejection. More specifically, we try to avoid the rejection of others. In order to avoid the sting of the rejection of others, our inner voice stops us from taking action and causes us to reject ourselves. Similarly, when it comes to advancements in your job or taking chances with relationships or self-improvement in other ways or accomplishments or treatments, etc., we are afraid someone is going to tell us that we are not good enough. We are afraid we won't stack up. So, really, we reject ourselves first. We tell ourselves we're not good enough so we don't have to hear it from somebody else.

We do this in order to give ourselves a perverse feeling of control. If we don't engage in these conversations, then we know what the outcome will be. We all have a psychological need for control and sometimes we achieve that end in a manner that ultimately does more harm than good.

This also demonstrates the benefit of meditation. It helps you to be more self-aware. You're able to separate your thoughts from who you are. It helps you to also pay attention to your thoughts and not get caught up in them.

A fundamental tenet of CBT is that what we think dictates how we feel and how we behave. So if we think about the threats and start to catastrophize the situation, we will feel scared and anxious; then we will act like we are scared and anxious.

This explains why imposter syndrome is such a big issue in our society today. With imposter syndrome, our internal voice tells us we can't succeed or we don't have what it takes. This leads us to have a disproportionate focus on our deficiencies, the risks, and our fears. This results in us holding back and not taking advantage of opportunities.

Our deficiencies are often magnified when we look at others. Especially with the advent of social media, we can only see their polished exteriors and it makes our flaws even more salient. This leads us to become convinced that they are legitimate and we are illegitimate. Imposter syndrome is paralyzing because it will cause you to avoid the potential embarrassment and humiliation that comes along with being exposed as an imposter to the world.

That's why we need to recognize that we are connected to the universal human experience. You are not the only person who feels this way; other people feel this way, too. As I'm writing this book, I'm feeling this way. The difference is that I've come to terms with the reality that I need to take action *despite* that feeling.

My goal with everything I do is to find my limit. I'm always trying to answer the question of how good I am. I will never know the answer to that question if I allow myself to fail before I even begin.

Imposter syndrome was at its height as I was preparing for my TEDx Talk, "Finding Confidence in Conflict." A mixtape of *Kwame's Greatest Insecurities* played on repeat in my mind. I felt vulnerable, exposed, scared, stupid, and unworthy. The negative voice in my head worked overtime to make sure I didn't step onto that stage.

Over the years, I've learned to question my emotions and act *in spite of* the fear. I've found that practice and rehearsal are the best antidotes for fear. I honed the content of my talk for about 10 hours per week for 12 weeks. The month leading up to the talk, I gave the speech from memory five to 10 times per day. I would wake up every morning at 5 am and, as I was getting dressed to go to the gym, I would say the speech backward, line by line. I practiced as much as I could, prepared as much as I could, and I came to terms with this reality: I have put myself in the best position for success. There isn't anything else I could've done differently to be more prepared than I am right now. Because of this, I am OK with failure because at least now I know my limit.

My solution to imposter syndrome is to shift my focus from the fear of failure to the fear of regret. It's okay to be afraid; just make sure you're afraid of the right thing. Fear can be a great motivator. In my mind, when I'm presented with these opportunities I'm afraid of failure the entire time and I want to quit. However, at the same time, when I'm about to quit I take a deathbed perspective. I ask myself, "Will I regret it if I don't take this opportunity?" If the answer is yes, then I take action.

We should look at difficult conversations the exact same way. The best things in life often lie on the other side of difficult conversations. This is especially true in the workplace. Imposter syndrome will cause you to question your worth and whether or not you deserve it. It will hold you back. That's when we need to ask ourselves whether or not we'll regret not having the difficult conversation. If the answer is yes, then you need to take action.

Fear of Awkwardness

"Awkwardness is an incongruence between what's happening and what we think should happen." This belief of what should be happening is governed more by our *perception* of what's happening than what's actually happening. This incongruence leads to emotional discomfort and we fear it will lead to social isolation.[16]

Early humans needed to remain part of the group in order to survive. This led to a hypersensitivity of social ostracization. This is why today conversations about religion or politics are seen as socially treacherous. Although we are more sophisticated and our society has developed to a point where we could still survive on our own, we still hold a deathlike fear of isolation.

One time I was representing a client who was buying a business. The business owner was eager to sell and my client was eager to buy. The problem was that the numbers weren't working out.

My client was getting nervous and said, "I'm friends with this guy. I don't want to push back and have him think I'm a cheap bastard."

I responded by saying, "That doesn't give him the right to actually *be* a cheap bastard. Don't worry. I'll be the bad guy and you can just sit back and let me handle this."

Did we get a deal? No. The numbers simply wouldn't work. However, my client and the other side were still good friends at the end of the process because of the way everyone handled the situation. The discomfort she was feeling was ultimately unwarranted because we were able ask for what we wanted without negatively impacting the relationship.

The first step in any negotiation is the ask. People often fail at this point because they don't want to look greedy or needy. This perception is threatening because in society it never looks good for you to look greedy. We need to live together as a community and people who are seen as greedy could be ostracized because people in the community don't see greedy people as providing enough value relative to what they demand. With regard to looking needy, people don't want others to look at them and assume that the reason you are asking for so much is because you don't have anything. This is our ego talking.

Making a request in a difficult conversation comes off as greedy only if you do it improperly. If you approach the other party respectfully, use Compassionate Curiosity, and justify your request with legitimate, objective criteria, people will not be offended by what you ask for. If you ask for something completely legitimate and the other person gets offended, that is their problem, not yours. You are only responsible for your behavior, not theirs.

With regard to the fear of looking needy, it's actually the people who have the most that ask for the most. Time after time, we see that the affluent have a mindset that leads them to make more aggressive requests. There are a lot of potential reasons for this. It may be due to the fact that they have a higher sense of self and make requests that are commensurate with their perceived self-worth. It may be due to the fact that their savvy led to their current affluence and they are simply following their recipe for success. Whatever the reason, their willingness to ask for what they want *is not* an indication of being needy or weak.

We often make the mistake of projecting our fears and worries onto the other party, which usually ends with us predicting an unbearably painful interaction. We make inaccurate assumptions about how they would respond emotionally to the situation and we're afraid of how they will feel or perceive us during and after the conversation. You'll find that, in most cases, our imagination manufactures a future that is far worse than reality. The Compassionate Curiosity Framework provides you with a model to lessen the likelihood of this awkwardness and discomfort when the conversation happens, which makes it more likely for you to engage. You'll know how to approach people in a manner that will alleviate the negative emotions on both sides of the equation.

Fear of the Perceived Lack of Control

Flying is, without a doubt, the safest way to travel. According to one study, there is "one fatal accident for every 16 million flights."17 On the other hand, "more than 32,000 people are killed and 2 million are injured each year from motor vehicle crashes."18 With this glaring discrepancy, why, then, are people more afraid of flying than driving?

It all comes down to your perception of control (and sometimes altitude). Most of the time when you're driving, you're behind the wheel or you're with someone you know. Even with Uber and Lyft, you at least get to see the driver's name and rating.

One of the biggest hurdles for artificial intelligence is its ability to mimic the human ability to process social situations. Each social decision we make is based on our history, which is comprised of thousands of other social interactions, the cultural norms of society, and a myriad of other considerations.[19] Human interaction is endlessly complex and it becomes even more complex when you add an element of conflict.

Thus, many people also struggle with the inherent unpredictability of conflict. It feels as though you have little control over the other party and the outcome. This perceived lack of control leads to anxiety. As a result, people choose not to engage in difficult conversations because the prospect of losing control is too much to handle.

However, the reality is that engaging in these difficult conversations is what puts you in the position to have the *most* possible control under the circumstances because you are being more proactive. Indecision and inaction cede control to outside forces. Consistently engaging in these difficult conversations with this framework gives you more control than you ever had.

One of the most beautiful things about the Compassionate Curiosity Framework is that even though you are controlling the conversation, you conduct the conversation in a way that gives the other side the illusion of control. By giving them the opportunity to speak and express themselves, they feel like they have more power as well.

Building the habit of engaging in these difficult conversations through Compassionate Curiosity will give you more control than you ever had in your personal and business relationships.

Anxiety

"Don't believe everything you think."

The power of the human imagination is incredible. Think of JK Rowling's contribution to literature. The Harry Potter series is 4,224 pages and 1,084,170 words. Harry Potter, his friends, Hogwarts, and the elaborate battle with Lord Voldemort originated completely from the mind of a single human being. It's really quite remarkable. It is an entirely fictional, fantastical tale that never really happened and will never happen. And yet she has the power to make Hogwarts seem very real to millions of people the world over.

Our minds work in the same way when we are feeling anxiety. We author incredible works of dark fiction and the majority of these terrible stories we invent will likely never happen. We expend an awful lot of cognitive energy creating these stories. Our mind is a lot like the news in this way —it is hyper-focused on the negative and sensational. The key difference between us and JK Rowling is that we believe our stories and they put us in a state of paralyzing fear.

Don't believe everything that you think. Most of time, these stories stem from a limited piece of information. We take that piece of information and manufacture an elaborate story that is most likely to lean negative.

The amygdala cannot distinguish between reality and fiction. Because of that, when we worry and go through these terrible scenarios in our minds, we will respond with the same fight, flight, or freeze response we would have if it actually happened.[20]

"Anxiety is an emotion characterized by feelings of tension, worried thoughts and physical changes like increased blood pressure."[21]

If you are afraid that a difficult conversation will be awkward, you will worry about it for hours before the conversation. This worry will inhibit your performance and result in the conversation being awkward when it didn't have to be. In this case, the fear is the mother of the very event you spent time worrying about. This is called anticipatory anxiety and it acts like a self-fulfilling prophecy.[22]

As it relates to difficult conversations, the worry that comes with anxiety "causes you to expand the problems and at the same time it causes you to constrict or limit the solutions."[23]Creativity is a critical part of collaborative negotiation because, in order to think outside the box, your mind must be in a state that is capable of considering a variety of solutions. This is why it's imperative to train your brain to see conflict as an opportunity. It will decrease your anxiety and increase your creativity. Thus, when we are presented with a conflict, we need to ask ourselves, "Where is the opportunity?" My goal is to always be able to finish this sentence: *This is an opportunity to...*

Anxiety comes from uncertainty. We don't know exactly what is coming next, so we worry about it. Most of the time, this worry comes in the form of the manufacture of ever-escalating worst-case scenarios. As this is happening, we trick ourselves into believing that this worry is productive because we are thinking about the situation beforehand.

How many times have you looked back on your life, grateful for the time you spent worrying? Most likely, the answer is never. When your mind races, it is your brain trying to find an explanation for the feelings in your body. That's why it feels like it is so out of control.

The majority of things that we worry about don't come to fruition after it is all said and done. However, that horrible fiction in our mind is exactly what prevents us from performing effectively or engaging at all. We allow our imaginations to prevent us from making the best of reality. In the end, we are left with our imagination and the absurdities of what we thought would happen. However, we are also left frustrated with the way we performed. Ultimately, we are left with regrets.

There is a difference between worry and preparation. This is why Compassionate Curiosity not only tells you what you need to focus on, but it also tells you what you need to ignore, both before and during the conversation. This helps to quiet your mind and put you in a cognitive state that is primed for performance.

Solutions for These Emotional and Psychological Barriers

**"Emancipate yourself from mental slavery.
None but ourselves can free our mind."
Bob Marley**

A great way to reduce the fear and anxiety you feel in these conversations is to visualize the following scenarios:

1. What will your life look like if you don't have this conversation?

2. What will your life look like if you have this conversation and it goes poorly? Would you be able to recover?

3. What will your life look like if you have this conversation and it goes okay?

4. What will your life look like if you have this conversation and it goes really well?

There's an important limit to this exercise. We need to be intentional about shortening the timeline of our extrapolations. Sometimes we worry about things that are so far into the future that we cannot be expected to accurately predict what is about to happen.[24] The further into the future we go, the more unknowns there are. This is problematic because unknowns create anxiety.

The purpose of going through this mental exercise is to help you recognize that even if this doesn't go well, you will still survive because you still have options. They might not be the best options, but they are options nonetheless. Understanding these options and having a greater appreciation of your resilience and ability to recover from failure is a key to becoming more confident in these conversations.

One of the most powerful things in a negotiation is the willingness to walk away from a bad deal. If your needs aren't being met, you know you have options and you won't feel pressured to push forward and try to force a yes when it is becoming clear that no is actually the right answer.

Negotiation isn't the art of deal making; it's the art of deal discovery. You're coming together with the other party to see if a deal is feasible. If it's not feasible, then you will exercise your other options.

When you go through this exercise, it will reduce your fear and anxiety because you will be able to see your possible life outcomes through your mind's eye. Recognizing that all of these options are survivable will make you more likely to act. Numerous studies have demonstrated that athletes who engage in visualization are consistently able to improve their performance and lower anxiety. However, this only works if you actually take the time to close your eyes and vividly see the story unfold in your mind. Simply answering the questions quickly and logically won't have the same beneficial impact on your emotions.

Mentally rehearsing an action is second-best to actually doing it. When it comes to difficult conversations, rehearsing in this way will help you to preview your emotional responses to the difficult conversation. After you visualize the person on the other side and you actually see your response, you can change the way you approach the conversation as necessary.

During the weeks leading up to my TEDx Talk, "Finding Confidence in Conflict," I visualized myself walking on stage and giving my speech. I did it so many times that by the time I actually presented, it felt familiar. I felt like I'd been there before and, even though I was speaking in front of a theater packed with 1,300 people, I felt relaxed and calm. It was a surreal experience.

Replace Worry with Preparation

Competence breeds confidence. The more you prepare, the more confident you will become.

Worry and anxiety often come about as a result of a lack of information. Your anxiety will decrease if you take the time to learn as much as possible about the other side and the situation.

This is because knowledge reduces the unknown. This is why it's beneficial to utilize a systematic approach to negotiation preparation and why a guide is included in your workbook. Remember you can download a free copy at www.AmericanNegotiationInstitute. com/workbook.

Mindfulness and Stress Reduction

Mindfulness is awareness and attention devoted solely to the moment. Mindful awareness as it relates to our emotions means that we acknowledge and recognize our emotions *without judgment.*

When we judge our emotions, we risk being taken down an unhelpful and unhealthy emotional pathway. This distracts us from the task at hand and can lead to the exacerbation of an already problematic emotional state.

As a Caribbean American, I have an affinity for the ocean. I can spend hours enjoying its splendor. One thing I learned at an early age is that you can't fight the waves because they will easily overpower you. Your only option is to let the wave flow over you and wait for it to pass.

Emotions are like waves. Don't fight them; feel them. Our body will naturally move toward homeostasis. The emotions typically come on strong and then slowly start to dissipate.[25] If you actively fight against the wave, you will lose and you will have a bad time losing.

If you are feeling a particularly high amount of stress in these conversations, finding ways to lower your overall baseline levels of stress in your life will be an important thing to do.[26] Here are four ways I've lowered my overall stress and have thus improved my performance in difficult conversations:

Meditation

I use the meditation application called Headspace because I find that my mind wanders without that constant guidance. Meditation has helped me reduce stress and worry, improved my focus, improved my mood, and quieted my mind. It also helps me sleep if my thoughts are racing. Who is in charge, the thinker or the thought? These negative thoughts come about organically. Your mind goes on autopilot but they are your thoughts. You need to regain control. Even though these thoughts happen, you can control your behavior.

Working Out

I originally started working out five days a week for the TEDx Talk, but after a few weeks I became addicted. When you work out, your body fills with natural opioids called endorphins, which make you feel good and lower your stress. It also gave me more energy so I could remain alert for longer periods throughout the day.

Scheduling Fun

Fun is one of the best ways to relieve stress and clear your mind. As I got older, opportunities for organic fun started to disappear. Because of this, I schedule my fun and I use my Instagram account as my fun journal to hold myself accountable.

Sleeping and Napping

Sleep plays an important role in emotional regulation. Sleep is better than caffeine because caffeine simply keeps you awake while sleep repairs your brain and improves cognitive function.

All of these things help me to maintain equanimity under duress in these difficult conversations.

Cognitive Reappraisal

I used to be terrified of public speaking. One time in high school, I was asked to read the announcements before an assembly. It went so poorly that one of my friends said that he couldn't tell if I was crying or talking.

My particular stress response to speaking in public included an elevated heart rate, heavy perspiration, and vocal constriction. I would then interpret that sensation as fear. However, if I won an award, saw an attractive person, or watched my favorite team win a championship, I would have a similar physical response. I would then interpret that same sensation as excitement.

Cognitive appraisal is your interpretation of a situation. Cognitive *reappraisal* is changing your interpretation of that situation. I decided to see the opportunity in these situations instead of the threat. I decided that whenever I started to perspire, my heart started to race, and I felt vocal constriction, it was a sign that I was excited, not scared. That made all the difference.

The body has a limited set of physiological responses to stress and anxiety. You may struggle to control those automatic responses, but you can control the way you interpret them. Seeing these conversations as an opportunity instead of a threat will help you to improve your performance when it matters most.

Think about an athlete when they work out. We often don't work out because we don't like the pain that comes along with working out, but those other people learn to embrace the pain. Feel the burn, feel the pump. They feel the same way—it hurts them the same way it hurts us—but they look at that pain differently. It is like a mark of achievement. It's a trophy they have earned. They feel the same pain, but move toward it, whereas you might move away from it.

Difficult conversations provide you with the opportunity to:

- Get more of what you want
- Avoid things you don't want
- Strengthen relationships
- Practice and improve your abilities for the next difficult conversation

Exposure Therapy

Exposure therapy is a tool therapists use to help patients overcome phobias, which includes exposing the patient to the fear-inducing stimulus in a controlled environment. With time, the duration and intensity of the exposure slowly increases until the patient overcomes the crippling fear.

Exposure therapy was the single best thing I did to overcome my fears and become more confident in these difficult conversations. I'll share that story in the next chapter.

Chapter 3

MINDSET

"Life isn't about finding yourself. Life is about creating yourself."[27]

Mindset can be defined as a fixed mental attitude or disposition that predetermines a person's responses to and interpretations of situations.[28]

Our behaviors spring from our attitudes. Thus, the goal here is to change your attitude as it relates to these difficult conversations because this will lead to positive behavioral change. This attitude change isn't limited to your perspective on difficult conversations; it extends to include your attitude toward yourself, others, and the possible outcomes of the conversation.

This is why we're addressing your personal psychological and emotional barriers and your mindset *before* we dig deeply into the Compassionate Curiosity Framework. Our negative mindsets create self-fulfilling prophecies, which are "beliefs that come true because we are acting as if it is already true."[29]

For example, if you think of conflict as a combative proceeding, you are more likely to interpret the neutral things that are said as threatening. As a result, you might respond with unwarranted levels of aggression, which leads the other side to reciprocate by being defensive or aggressive. This causes the conversation to spiral into an unproductive, unpleasant, and needlessly combative interaction, entirely due to your improper mindset.

Let's take the same situation and change the mindset. What happens if you instead see these conflicts as an opportunity to learn? Since your goal is to learn, you'll ask more questions and because you actually care about the answers, you'll listen to the responses. They'll feel heard and now they will reciprocate by listening to you. The conversation is more likely to stay productive and you are more likely to have a favorable result. This subtle shift in mindset changes the process *and* the outcome. You didn't need to learn any high-level strategy or tactics in order to achieve this success. All of that positivity flowed directly from your change in mindset.

With these difficult conversations, discomfort is guaranteed. That's why it's important to remember that we don't have these conversations because they feel good or because they are easy; we have these conversations because they are worth it.

This is why you need to trust the process. In order to be successful, you need to embrace that feeling of discomfort and wear it as a badge of honor. It's a signal that you're on the right track.

Lacking control is scary. The Compassionate Curiosity Framework gives you the most control you could possibly have in your relationships and negotiations. Why? Instead of ceding control to the other party or to time, you're being proactive by taking committed action. The conversation is taking place on your terms and, because of your new skills and mindset, you are equipped to steer the conversation in a productive direction.

We need to develop a sense of urgency with regard to the improvement of this skill. The time to improve is now. You can't wait until the "perfect time" because that is just another avoidance strategy. Be comfortable with imperfect action. Later will always seem like a better time to do the difficult things in life.[30]

There's an old Chinese Proverb that says,"The best time to plant a tree was 20 years ago. The second-best time is now." The best time to change your mindset is *today*. Assuming that your career is moving in an upward trajectory, the stakes are higher now than they ever have been before. This means it's more important now than ever to engage in these difficult conversations in a thoughtful way in order to put yourself in the best position for success. The best things in life lie on the other side of difficult conversations. Thus, taking the time to improve this skill will put you on track to living your best possible life. Similarly, if you continue on this upward trajectory, the stakes are going to be even higher next year. If you take the time to practice and improve, you're going to be better equipped to handle those higher-stakes conversations.

An important part of embracing this new mindset is changing the way we talk about ourselves. People often say things like "I'm a horrible negotiator," "I'm a people-pleaser," "I'm a doormat," and "I don't know what I'm doing." When they say these things, they make the critical mistake of labeling themselves in fixed, concrete terms. However, the reality is these are transient states. It's like a white belt in karate looking at the black belt and saying, "I'll never be able to do that; I'm just a white belt." Then why are you here?

It's not fair to criticize yourself for being at the beginning of a journey. It doesn't make any sense. It's like getting in your car for a road trip and, as you start the car, saying, "I'm never going to make it there. I'm still in my driveway." The beginning stages of a journey are just a part of the journey. If you simply haven't started your journey yet, that's okay. Let this book be the start for you. This is the first step in your journey to mastery.

Remember, the goal here is mastery, not simply improvement. If you read this book and implement its techniques, you will undoubtedly improve, but don't get complacent. You can always get better. I'm still getting better and I will be for decades. I look at my journey as the pursuit of perfection while recognizing that perfection is an unattainable goal. This leads to constant improvement.

This chapter is a reflection of my philosophy on human interactions, both personal and business. It permeates how I view *all* human interaction. This consistency of approach helps me to navigate my most difficult conversations in a way that puts me in the best position to get what I want without jeopardizing relationships.

For example, this philosophy makes me look at every interaction with my two-year-old son, Kai, as an opportunity to teach him how to interact with others, resolve conflict, persuade, and communicate. I am about 5 feet taller than Kai and weigh almost 200 pounds more than him. I could simply force him to do whatever I wanted, but I'm not going to do that because that's not how I want him to navigate the world.

If a child grows up in an atmosphere where the only tools to gain compliance are coercion and punishment, it will make it more difficult for them to manage conflict effectively and persuade as they get older. This is because the only tools at their disposal would be the carrot-and-stick approach, which can only go so far when it comes to having difficult conversations.

Even though it takes a lot of patience and time, I believe it is a worthwhile investment because, as he gets older, his problems will become more complex. By equipping him with the ability to manage conflict and negotiate, he will be better able to solve his own problems verbally, which will make parenting easier in the future, I hope.

This mindset in the parenting realm not only helps the children; it also helps you, the parent. My most frustrating (and rewarding) interactions are with Kai. Everything else feels easy if I start my day with a "hostile negotiation" with my son.

Reconceptualizing Key Attitudes

Fully embracing this new mindset will require you to think differently about common, problematic attitudes.

The Fear of Failure vs. The Fear of Regret

We often make the mistake of focusing too narrowly on the outcome of the specific conversation. This causes us to see the outcome in a binary way—we're either winning or losing. Not surprisingly, since humans are predisposed to focus on the negative, we focus on the prospect of losing, which leads to the crippling fear of failure.

These interactions and conversations are complex. When you expand the scope of your analysis, you'll see that the ramifications of the conversation with regard to outcome and process extend far into the future.

Thus, when it comes to making the decision as to whether or not I act, I take a longer-term perspective and ask myself the following questions:

- Will you regret failing to have this conversation next week?

- Will you regret failing to have this conversation next month?

- Will you regret failing to have this conversation next year?

As I started having these internal dialogues, I realized that my substantive concerns give way to my psychological concerns the further I extend the analysis. This means that in the majority of cases, the substantive outcome is more important in the short term but the psychological outcome is more important in the long term.

This is because every time I choose to engage in these difficult conversations, I am improving my skills and becoming more confident in conflict. With each interaction, I am becoming the confident negotiator I always wanted to be.

Consistent Comfort vs. Post Traumatic Growth

We know that the difficulty you experience during difficult conversations makes you stronger; however, it's easy to overlook the fact that the opposite is also true. Failing to put yourself in difficult situations makes you weaker. We want to minimize resistance to make our lives easier, but we don't realize that we're doing this at the expense of our strength.

If you're not feeling productive discomfort, you're not growing. For example, if you're not feeling productive discomfort in your job, then you're not advancing. If you're not feeling productive discomfort in your relationships, then they are likely stagnating. Thinking of difficult conversations in this way will make it more likely for you to adopt a mindset that's eager to move toward conflict despite the pain.

Winning vs. Workable

I almost always include some kind of role play or custom negotiation simulation in my seminars. What's interesting is that people will feel they got a good deal until they hear the deal that somebody else got. One participant even said, "I thought I got a good deal but apparently I got smoked!"

Success and failure in these negotiations are subjective and largely relative. What we find in these simulations and in real life is that there is a wide range of possible deals that fall with- in the zone of agreement. It's impossible to know everything about the other party in particular and the situation in general to know whether or not you got the *best deal.*

Therefore, don't focus on the best deal because there's no way for you to know whether or not you got it. It's more productive to focus on workable deals. Ask yourself if the outcome meets your needs and is palatable to the other side. If it is, then congratulations! You've achieved a workable outcome.

Being Right vs. Being Persuasive

Another thing that makes argumentation and persuasion difficult is the fact that there is no objectivity to the weight of the points or arguments you make. On the basketball court, if you shoot from here it's worth two points and if you shoot from there it's worth three points. There is objectivity to the scoring. When it comes to difficult conversations, however, there usually isn't an unbiased tribunal that makes decisions, nor is there any way to objectively determine winners and losers.

This subjectivity demonstrates why negotiation is both art and science. We learn the science in order to improve the art we produce. We can't simply rely on facts and logic to win the day.

Truth vs. Stories

After years of negotiating and mediating, I've learned something very interesting. In 99% of the cases, both sides have something in common. This is true whether it is a negotiation, a mediation, or an argument between friends or loved ones. What do they have in common? Both sides think they are right. How can that be possible?

Mediation has given me a unique opportunity to look behind the veil of these conflicts and see the perspectives of both sides. We should try our best to do the same thing in our everyday conflicts. We need to try to understand the perspective of the other side. You don't need to agree with what they're saying but you can seek to understand how they came to believe what they believe.

In our education system, we are taught that there is always a right answer. The thing that makes negotiation so difficult is that there is no such thing as a right answer. Your confidence in negotiation will rise significantly when you come to terms with the fact that there will always be an element of uncertainty no matter how much you prepare. It's like driving. You can be a perfect driver and still get in an accident, but that shouldn't stop you from driving. It should, however, make you want to be as good of a driver as you possibly can be, with the goal of increasing the likelihood of a successful, safe trip. That is what we are trying to do here. We want to build skills to increase our likelihood of a successful outcome, while understanding that it is not entirely in our control.

The information age has made us intellectually lazy with regard to persuasion in difficult conversations. We make the mistake of thinking that information is all you need to win the day.

One of the most frustrating things that could possibly occur in these conversations is when we present facts and those facts are unable to persuade the other side. It feels as though the other side is impervious to our facts. When you're dealing with beliefs and emotions, you're going to need more than just facts; you're going to need the ability to persuade.

My goal here is to spread the inconvenient truth that truth is not enough to get you what you want. It doesn't matter if you're right. Being right and being persuasive are not the same thing.

As a mediator, I have the pleasure of being placed right in the center of some of the most vitriolic conflicts. I get to hear the "honest truth" about what happened from both parties in addition to why they have the moral high ground. These stories originate from the same set of facts; it's fascinating to see how different the stories end up being. There are a number of factors that lead to the discrepancies:

- Memory is fallible: Memory begins to decay immediately after the event.[31]

- Memory is malleable: Memories change every time they are recalled.[32]

- Memory is impressionable: Memories begin to be recalled in a manner more favorable to you because of self-serving biases.

Thus, often times we have two parties arguing vigorously over their warped, self-serving memories.

In the majority of these conflicts, it's between two people who are the main witnesses to whatever happened. Because of our different perspectives and self-serving biases we will interpret the exact same thing in the manner that is most favorable to us: the manner that is most favorable to us in terms of consequence and outcome and the matter that is most favorable to us in terms of self-perception and self-esteem. The other person is doing the exact same thing. So, in a situation where there are only two people and they each see the situation through their own eyes, there is no objective, unbiased interpretation of what happened.

This begs the question, what is truth? Then, if there is no truth, then what is right and wrong? When we enter these conversations looking for truth and right and wrong, we are basing our argument on things that don't truly exist in this particular situation.

Don't think of it in terms of true and false; think in terms of stories. Due to the positivity bias, we will almost always see ourselves as the hero of the story, but we need to recognize that we also play a role as the villain in the stories of others.

Considering this reality, we recognize the difficulty in coming to these conversations from a position of right versus wrong, good versus evil. If that is the pre-conceived notion, you begin the argument from a place of contention by recasting them or forcing them to recast themselves as the villain in their own mind, which is difficult, if not impossible, to do.

We need to focus on our goal. Is our goal to get them to recast themselves in this way? No. Our goal is to have a conversation that changes behavior. At best, what we can get them to do is to recast themselves as misunderstood or misinformed. What they did wasn't wrong or what they said wasn't wrong; it was just misunderstood. Or what they did or said was wrong be- cause of misinformation. Had they known this information, they would have behaved differently. Attempting to recast them in this way gives them an opportunity to save face. They don't need to become the villain in order for you to get what you need and want out of the situation.

Thinking of facts as stories helps us avoid getting married to our rigid perspective of what did or did not happen and allows us to be more open to hear what other people say. When we understand that we are biased toward ourselves and we might see things improperly, we can see the benefit of listening to their story. This approach gives us one of the most important ingredients of effective listening—humility.

It also helps us to avoid judging the other side so harshly.

We aren't going into the conversation believing that they are lying to us. We respect that their story is the way they see it. In the end, we may not agree with the facts of the past, but if we engage in the conversation thoughtfully, we still have a chance to co-create an acceptable future.

This is why I avoid talking about the past and who's right and who's wrong in difficult conversations. It's unclear. A lot of times, we not only don't know what happened, but there is no way for us to find out what happened.

My technique for overcoming this is to utilize future-focused problem-solving. When using this technique, I'm willing to sacrifice the past in order to win the future. The way I do this is by changing the grammatical tense of the conversation. If they want to argue about the past, I let them know that I'm listening and then I say something like, "You have a great point there. Given that, what do you think we can do to make sure we can avoid this in the future?"

This works because it reorients their focus to the future, which is more productive. We can change the future; we can't change the past. Anger and resentment can be found in the past and the present; however, since the future is yet to be determined, it's less likely that conversations that discuss the future will carry the same emotional baggage. This approach will help you to avoid a significant number of needless squabbles.

Talent vs. Skills

Your ability to perform in these difficult conversations is a skill, not a talent. People look at me as an attorney and say, "You're a great negotiator." They look at me as a mediator and say, "You're comfortable in conflict." The reality is that I was profoundly bad at all of those things; however, by following the steps in this book, I was able to overcome and excel. You can, too.

Threat vs. Opportunity

When people ask you what you learned from this book tell them this, "**conflict is an opportunity.**"

One of the biggest emotional issues we face in these conversations is the fact that people conflate conflict and combat. Combat is an altercation with the mutual goal of doing damage. Conflict is an opportunity for understanding and connection. When you think of conversations as combat, not only are you trying to inflict damage, but you also are scared because you believe that you are likely going to take damage as well. It is difficult to be at your best with this kind of stress.

We need to develop opportunity-based thinking (OBT). With OBT, you analyze the situation and look for the opportunities that are provided by the conflict. Conflict provides us with the opportunity to:

- Connect

- Learn about others

- Learn about ourselves

- Strengthen and maintain valuable relationships

- Identify and remove malignant relationships with minimal damage

- Get more of what we want

- Avoid undesirable outcomes

- Improve our skill, ability, and poise in difficult conversations

When we see conflict as an opportunity, it allows us to navigate the conversation without the threat of inevitable pain. We can respect that they currently see the situation one way and we see the situation another way. We use that understanding as we take advantage of the opportunity to learn from each other. We should seek to learn about their emotional challenges, substantive challenges, and goals. If you start with this foundation, you position yourself to be able to work with the other side to create a future that is acceptable to both parties.

Every social interaction provides us with a strategic opportunity. I see negotiation as a never-ending game of chess where you're constantly positioning yourself and others to put yourself in the best position possible to accomplish your long-term goals. Sometimes it's difficult to see the strategic opportunity in these interactions, especially if we aren't thinking clearly because of stress or because the interaction seems too mundane or unimportant. In these cases, challenge yourself to finish this sentence: "This conversation is an opportunity to..."

This exercise is the heart of OBT. When you use OBT, you are considering your ultimate goal. You're asking yourself, "What is the point of this conversation?" This helps you figure out which conflicts are worth your time. When you answer this question, you might find that your only goal is to make somebody feel bad or show that you are right. You might recognize that your goal isn't legitimate.

Not only has OBT helped me navigate the business world and social circles more effectively and strategically, it also helps me in everyday situations. For example, sometimes I am running late when I get my son, Kai, ready for school in the morning. I might be jogging into the daycare and Kai might stop and point at a bug and say, "Look daddy! A bug!" Instead of getting upset like I did in the past, now I stop and think to myself, "Kwame, this is an opportunity to practice my patience. This is an opportunity to show Kai that I value and respect his interests, even if I am in a hurry." The benefits of adopting this mindset extend far beyond your ability to perform in difficult conversations.

Condemnation vs. Curiosity

Condemnation only exists with a sense of self-right-eousness and a monopolization of the moral high ground. This leads to the vilification of others. I'm right and we disagree, which means that you must be wrong. This leads us to blaming.

You can't be curious if you are blaming, because if you are blaming that means you've already come to a clear conclusion in your mind. What is the purpose of further investigation? Even if we go through the motions of asking questions, with this mindset, those questions won't sound as though they are meant to seek true answers; they will sound as though they are meant to get convictions. You will sound like a prosecutor asking questions to which you already know the answer. You are only asking those questions to entrap the person on the other side.

If you approach a situation with a sense of certainty or condemnation, you will find it almost impossible to genuinely listen. You may pretend to listen or listen only for vulnerabilities in their facts or logic for you to attack. We need to learn to replace condemnation with curiosity.

My goal in every conversation is to adhere to the 70/30 Rule of Negotiation. This rule holds that you should try to listen 70% of the time and speak only 30% of the time. I do this for four reasons:

1. Knowledge is power. This approach creates an information asymmetry in my favor, which gives me more power relative to them during the conversation

2. Control. Asking questions puts you in control of the direction of the conversation.

3. Comfort. They feel safe and comfortable when they are talking and know that I am listening. This allows them to trust me faster and makes them feel comfortable sharing more. It leads to the free flow of information and a strong working relationship.

When we have these difficult conversations, we need to be humble enough to recognize that people see things differently and their perspectives have value. There is going to be some information that only exists in their minds. The more information you have, the better able you will be to find new solutions.

When it comes to persuasion, it's important to remember that we can't convince anyone of anything. The best we can do is create an atmosphere that allows them to convince themselves. We can do that by structuring and sequencing our questions in a way that leads them down a path that makes it easy to change their minds without the fear of losing face.

One of the things that makes these conversations so difficult is our perpetual focus on ourselves. We are right, we are scared, etc. There's no consideration of the other side outside of our belief that they are wrong. What are they feeling? Why do they feel that way? Why do they think that way? Replace your spirit of certainty and need to be right with a desire for understanding. Anxiety is a self-focused emotion. Even when we think of others when we're worried or anxious, we're only considering their thoughts, wants, and needs *as they relate to ourselves.*

It takes courage to be willing to seemingly take your hand off of the steering wheel in these conversations by speaking less and listening more. It takes courage to be willing to suspend your personal agenda in order to gain a better understanding of your friend, spouse, or colleague. However, this approach comes with a hidden benefit—it takes pressure off of you. You don't need to be a brilliant orator in order to be persuasive; you just need to be curious. You need to be willing to learn and understand. The issue of not knowing what to say starts to go away when you are saying less.

Now vs. Later

We often make the mistake of unnecessarily delaying these difficult conversations. We constantly make   excuses as to why we shouldn't do it today. These lies we tell ourselves are the rationalization of the primitive fear response. We do this not only to avoid discomfort, awkwardness, and temporary pain, but also because we believe that, for whatever reason, we will be better equipped to handle the situation in the future.[33]

The reality is that fear feeds on time. If you are afraid of having a conversation now and you avoid it, you provide your fear the time it needs to grow. With every hour, day, and week that passes, the complexity and emotional baggage associated with the conflict gets bigger and scarier. Thus, putting off a conversation will actually make you *more* emotionally compromised.

However, sometimes delaying the conversation is necessary for legitimate strategic purposes or because it's simply not feasible to have the conversation immediately. When you are unable to engage in the conflict immediately, you need to schedule it. Set a deadline and stick to it and hold yourself accountable. If you decide to put a deadline on having the difficult conversation, it's often in your best interest to let the other person know it's coming so they don't feel ambushed.

Conflict as a Threat vs. Conflict as a Symptom

A symptom is "any phenomenon or circumstance accompanying something and serving as evidence of it."[34] In medicine, it serves as a signal that alerts you to a deeper physical or mental issue. Similarly, conflict is a signal of deeper issues in a business or relationship.

When good medical professionals become aware of a symptom in a patient, they use it as an *opportunity to investigate*. They get curious instead of seeing it as a threat and avoiding it or pretending everything's okay. They ask questions and run tests to learn more in order to ultimately treat the malady. We need to become doctors of conflict. We need to recognize conflict as a symptom of an underlying problem in the relationship or the business deal and use it as an opportunity to investigate. When you couple this point with the reality that conflicts become scarier and more complicated with time, it makes it clear that time is of the essence when it comes to addressing any conflicts.

Confident vs. Intimidated

Intimidation can be defined as follows:

1. to make timid; to fill with fear.

2. to overwhelm or to be put in a state of awe, as through the force of personality or by superior display of wealth, talent, intelligence, status, etc.

3. to force into or deter from some action by inducing fear.

There are going to be instances where we have to have a difficult conversation with someone who intimidates us.

Being intimidated will have a negative impact on your ability to protect your interests and ultimately get what you want out of these difficult conversations.

The key to overcoming intimidation is to see the humanity in the person who intimidates you *and* see the humanity in yourself. In other words, intimidation makes them "more than" while at the same time makes you "less than." Thus, we need to bring our regard for them down to appropriate levels while at the same time bringing your regard for yourself up to appropriate levels.

If you are a person who is easily intimidated, you need to find an anchor that connects you to the humanity of the person who scares you. Here are two things that I do in order to find their humanity.

Everyone blinks

I want you to envision the person who intimidates you. They may have a higher status, they may be physically bigger, and they may have more resources. Additionally, they may be intentionally posturing and acting aggressively to emphasize their advantage over you. I want you to look into their imaginary eyes and don't break eye contact until you see them blink. This big, scary person just slid two small, delicate pieces of skin to moisten their tiny, little eyes. When I see them do this, I think it's kind of cute and makes me say t myself, "Awww, you're a human just like me!"

When I do this in the real conversation it has a number of benefits:

1. I'm less intimidated because I think they just did something cute.

2. It makes me more willing to listen and find more humanity inside of them.

3. It has the natural effect of keeping my eyes and head up, which signals confidence and helps me to avoid the submissive body language of lowering my gaze and bringing my chin closer to my chest.

4. It helps me to maintain eye contact.

Everyone was a baby

As the father of a two-year-old, I'm too familiar with tantrums. Tantrums often occur for two reasons:

1. A baby has a want or need but, due to physical limitations, is unable to satisfy those wants or needs themselves, which leads to frustration.

75

2. A baby has a want or need but, due to cognitive limitations, is unable to express those wants or needs, which leads to frustration.

Adults aren't much different. When someone is misbehaving, I try to envision them as a baby. I wonder what kind of difficult circumstances this person had to go through as a child that created the cacophony of undesirable personality traits I'm dealing with right now. Imagine that child struggling. When it comes down to it, we are all people trying to be happy and looking for love and acceptance. Sometimes, because of our upbringing, we go about it the wrong way. Imagine a difficult upbringing. As you see that young child struggling, it will cause you to empathize with the person. I assume that they are probably doing the best they can given their upbringing and beliefs.

This helps me to look at them with empathy. It's important to make sure you don't shift from empathy to pity.

Empathy is the recognition and appreciation of the thoughts, feelings, and attitudes of another. Pity is a negative emotion that comes about as the result of seeing the suffering, distress, or misfortune of another, *often leading one to give relief*. The critical difference between empathy and pity is that pity will tempt you to cede your position for *their benefit* because you feel bad for them. Empathy, on the other hand, allows you to see the situation from their point of view and respect their humanity while engaging in the conversation in a way that protects your interests.

Seeing and respecting your own humanity will be addressed in more depth in the following chapter on confidence. Self-confidence is the best antidote for intimidation.

Playing the Role You Want to Play vs. Playing the Role You Need to Play

Understanding your role in these conversations will bring a lot of clarity to the way you need to perform. Before every conversation, you need to ask yourself the following questions:

1. What parts of your identity or personality do you need to bring to the conversation in order to get the best outcome?

2. What part of your identity or personality do they expect to see during the conversation?

The goal is to bring the most persuasive parts of your *authentic self* to the conversation.

We all have various roles, characteristics, and attributes that are part of our authentic self. For example, I am a father, a husband, a lawyer, a friend, a brother, a son, a mentor, a mediator, an educator, and more. Each of these identities is within my authentic self.

However, that doesn't mean I bring *all* of myself to the table at the same time. Kwame the father wouldn't be as successful in a hostile negotiation with opposing counsel as Kwame the lawyer. Kwame the lawyer won't help my child navigate his tantrums. Therefore, we need to pick and choose the parts of our authentic self that would be best suited for this specific situation.

Chapter 4

How We See Ourselves

This new mindset will change the way we see the world. In particular, it will impact how we see ourselves, others, and the outcomes in these difficult conversations. Our new perspective will naturally lead to more favorable outcomes in these difficult conversations.

Understand Your Why

The only way you will adopt a new approach and make this significant life change is if you are able to connect this change to a very clear and powerful why. Answer the following questions for yourself:

- Why did you get this book?

- Why do you want to improve?

- Why are you having this specific conversation?

- Who benefits from my improved abilities?

"Those who have a 'why' to live, can bear with almost any 'how.'"[35] You have to ask yourself in general and in your specific situation, "What is my purpose? What is my goal?"

When you clearly articulate your purpose and goals you'll realize that difficult conversations are an unavoidable part of the equation. Your confidence will be bolstered by the strength of your convictions. The clearer your purpose, the more confidence you will have in yourself and your actions. We need to find the root of the matter.

Let's take a moment and think about the word root in a literal sense. The root systems of redwood trees, for example, "extend over one hundred feet from the base, intertwining with the roots of other redwoods. This increases their stability during strong winds and floods."36 Sometimes the root system is more impressive and complex than the tree itself. If you don't take the time to explore why you believe what you believe and want what you want, you're missing out on a lot of vital supplementation to your confidence stores. You can look to the root of your why for strength during your conversation.

This is not simply an intellectual exercise. Digging deeply into your psyche will provide you with a deeper understanding of yourself and the discussion at hand.

I coached an executive at a nonprofit who was in charge of fundraising but struggled to negotiate effectively. She wanted to become a better advocate for her organization but struggled to push hard enough to really move the needle.

I recognized that she was more motivated by relationships than by money. As a result, she was particularly sensitive to the risk of offending others and the sting of rejection. We decided that she needed a stronger why.

I asked her why she joined the organization. She said that she joined because she loves the mission and cares about the well-being of children. Then I asked her if she thought of a specific child when she thought about the organization's mission.

Her eyes lit up and she immediately said, "Mark! When he came into the organization he was at risk and struggling at school because of his family situation. Now his family is stable and he was able to raise his grades enough to get accepted to a community college."

"Do you have a picture of Mark and his family?" I asked.

"I'm sure I could find one."

I said, "Here's what I want you to do from now on when you're on these fundraising calls. I want you to put that picture on your desk and look at it throughout the conversation, especially when you feel resistance. This will help you focus on your purpose and you will put the needs of kids like Mark in front of your desire for comfort."

After that, she was able to raise significantly more money for her company. She achieved this before we even talked about specific strategies and tactics. This demonstrates the power of mindset. When she changed the way she thought about the situation and fully understood her purpose, she was able to move outside of her comfort zone in order to achieve her goals.

I find that this is particularly useful for people who work in helping professions or nonprofits, or have come from poverty. They experience a version of survivor's guilt where they constantly question why they are worthy of so much when there are good people who have so little. As a result, not only do they fail to advocate for what they deserve financially and professionally, they also feel a sense of guilt and self-directed moral condemnation if they do ask for more.

The reality is that depriving yourself doesn't create more for others. For people in this situation, finding the deeper values that live behind your requests is critical. You don't want a bigger salary just for the sake of having more money for yourself. There's deeper meaning. For example:

- *Why do you want more money?*

- I want more money because I want to buy a house.

- *Why do you want to buy a house?*

- I want to buy a house to give some stability to my husband and kids.

- *Why do you want more stability for your family?*

- Because I grew up in an unstable environment and sometimes we didn't know where we were going to sleep. Once we get that stability I'll have more money that I can use to help others.

- *How would you use your money to help others?*

- I would donate to social movements I believe in.

In other words, the person in this scenario really wanted more money to stabilize her family and change the world. When you look at it this way, it makes it a lot easier to make the ask.

Understanding your why is arguably more important in conflicts that lie outside of the realm of the business world. We have more resilience with work-related conflict because the payoff is clear—I'm enduring this stress and annoyance so I can get paid. It is more difficult for us to keep our cool in personal situations because the payoff is often unclear.

Ask yourself the following:

- Why do I care about the outcome of this conversation?

- What is the impact of a successful outcome?

- What are the ramifications of an unsuccessful outcome?

- Why do I have this relationship?

- What is the value to me and to the other person?

It's important to have a clear idea of your goals and why you are engaging in this conflict because it will give you the resilience and energy you need to push through.

Think Strategically

"Every move must have a purpose."[37]

Earlier this year I received an exciting notification from Chess.com, letting me know that I played my 10,000th game of chess. My chess obsession taught me to look at negotiation like a never-ending game of chess. If you're creative, there can be a strategic purpose behind every human interaction. If you manage these relationships effectively, it could result in you having a much easier time when difficult conversations inevitably arise.

Each interaction is, at minimum, an opportunity to invest in the relationship bank account. With each positive interaction, you are increasing the amount of goodwill they feel toward you. This will increase the likelihood that they will give you the benefit of the doubt in ambiguous situations and give you want you want when you need it. This is how you build a strong working relationship that is typified by trust. Trust is built by making consistent deposits in the relationship bank account through these mundane interactions.

Chess is all about positioning. You want to put yourself in the best position to take advantage of strategic opportunities. Similarly, when you build relationships, especially in the business world, you should ask yourself, "Am I putting myself in the best strategic position for success?" Before difficult conversations, I ask myself, "Based on my goals and current circumstances, what strategic approach would put me in the best position for success during this conversation?"

When you're in these conversations, your only goal is to make the best move you could possibly make given your current position. It doesn't make sense to lament about the mistakes you made in the past because that is not your current position.

That's a distraction. Recognize where you currently are. Recognize where you eventually want to go. Then make the best move to put you in a position to get there.

After this analysis you might find that your ability to persuade in the conversation at hand is limited. This occurs when there is a sizable gap between where you currently are and where you want to go using the tools of persuasion. In order to analyze the size of this gap, it's helpful to think of it in terms of persuasive weight.

Imagine you're working at a gym and you've been tasked with moving all of the free-weights, ranging from five pounds to one hundred twenty pounds, all the way to the other side of the building. How would you do it? You wouldn't try to move all of that weight at the same time, you would recognize that your only path to success was to make several trips.

This metaphor will help you to recognize that sometimes the best thing to do is to break a particularly difficult negotiation into a series of **micro-negotiations**. This is especially helpful if you are presented with surprising information in the middle of the conversation. Micro-negotiations help to lessen the persuasive weight by dispersing the burden of persuasion across multiple conversations.

Here's an example. Imagine your manager scheduled a meeting with you. You're excited about the prospect of this meeting because you believe that you've been performing well. You eagerly start going through the free salary negotiation guide that's included in your free downloadable workbook[38] to prepare. However, when you get into the meeting, you're shocked to discover that your manager is disappointed with your work and you won't be getting a raise this year.

This is where you need to gather yourself and re-evaluate your goals in the negotiation. You recognize that getting from where you are now in this conversation to a raise will be nearly impossible. The persuasive weight is too great. However, it's still possible to find value in this conversation.

Ask yourself, "Given this new information, what can I realistically get out of this conversation?" In this scenario, you feel as though your career and livelihood are being threatened and you're confused because you thought things were going well. As such, you might determine that the best-case scenario is for you to accomplish the following:

1. Leave the conversation without taking any more damage to your career;

2. Get as much information as possible to understand their perspective; and

3. Schedule a follow up meeting because you realize that achieving your ultimate goal in this conversation is highly unlikely.

Before and during difficult conversations, you need to ask yourself this question, "Given my current position, what is the best move I can make *right now*?" The words "right now" are an important part of the   equation because it helps you to focus on what is within your control and helps you to stay in the moment. You can't control the future, you can't change the past, but you can do something about the present. Focus your precious cognitive energy on the things you can control.

Negotiation strategy is an obsession for me. If you join our online course, you'll discover all of the best science-based negotiation and conflict resolution strategies for success in these difficult conversations.

Control

In order to increase your level of comfort in these difficult conversations, you need to come to terms with what you can and can't *completely* control. As a father, I've learned that there will be days where I say and do everything right and, despite my best efforts, Kai will still misbehave. Recognizing that it's not entirely my fault and there are forces beyond my control helps me to maintain my composure when he's acting up.

Similarly, we need to recognize that a significant portion of these interactions lies outside of our realm of control. Thus, we need to develop a narrow focus on what we actually *can* control in these difficult conversations.

Here is a non-exhaustive list of things you can control:

- Your level of preparation before the difficult conversation
- How you comport yourself during the conversation
- What you say during the conversation
- How you say what you say during the conversation
- Your mindset before and during the conversation

- Your willingness to listen

- Your level of curiosity

- Your patience

Here is a non-exhaustive list of things you can't *completely* control:

- Whether or not they agree

- Whether or not they are willing to make a deal

- Whether or not they listen

- How they comport themselves during the conversation

- Whether or not they treat you with respect

- Their level of aggression

I emphasize the word completely because, although you don't have complete control, you can approach the conversation in a way that has an impact on these things.

In order to change their behavior, you need to be in control of your own behavior. It starts with developing the appropriate mindset and preparing effectively for each of these conversations. You have to come to terms with the fact that *you* can never change somebody. *You* can never convince anyone of anything. The best thing you can do is to approach the conversation in a way that allows them to convince themselves.

Focus is a finite resource. Every iota of mental energy we allocate toward worrying about things that are outside of our control takes away mental energy we could give to things that are within our control.

Negotiation is like a dance. If you have two good dancers, you can have an enjoyable, aesthetically pleasing dance. However, if you have a bad partner who is hell-bent on being bad, you need to come to terms with the fact that this dance is going to be clunky, awkward, and unpleasant. There's simply no easy way around this. This is because we have free will. We have choices. No matter what you do or say, someone may still choose to act poorly and there's nothing you can do about it.

Chapter 5

How We See Others

**It only takes one person to improve the
quality of a relationship.**

Your first interaction with someone is the beginning of a
relationship. The quality of these relationship will be con-
tingent upon each party's ability to live up to the expectations of the other.

The cause of the breakdown of all relationships is the viola-
tion of expectations—I thought you would do or say this
but, in reality, you did or said that. The amount of disappointment, anger, and frustration we feel will be commensurate with the gap between our expectations and reality.
This helps to explain why negotiating the expectations of
the other party *as soon as possible* is one of the most important negotiations you can have over the course of the relationship.

You want to make sure you are all on the same page before
moving forward. For example, an executive at a malpractice insurance company, said that approximately 30% of
malpractice claims come as the result of unclear expectations between attorney and client.

We need to prioritize the discovery of the expectations of others and the revelation of our expectations *to* others. When we recognize a discrepancy, we have uncovered the topic of our next difficult conversation. You can then approach the process like any other negotiation or conflict— by using the Compassionate Curiosity Framework.

Relationship Tests

"Honest conflict is more socially valuable than dishonest harmony."[39]

The longest-running study of people found that the people who have strong relationships lived longer and had happier, healthier lives. "The people who were the most satisfied in their relationships at age 50 were the healthiest at age 80." Navigating conflict effectively and amicably can help us to repair, strengthen, and protect these critical relationships. The people who had healthy relationships still had conflicts, they just handled them in a healthy way.[40]

There are two important takeaways here:

1. Conflict is not indicative of a broken relationship. When done right, it is a signal of two or more people trying to make things better.

2. Conflict is the unsung hero of healthy relationships. It is the key to finding balance with others.

Conflict is an inevitable part of relationships. These conflicts are often typified by stress, frustration, and fear. These feelings and instances of conflict shouldn't be seen as a sign that something is wrong with you or something is wrong with the other person. The fact of the matter is that every relationship has a set failure point. Conflict provides us with the opportunity to potentially repair and rebuild these relationships once we reach that point of failure.

Life doesn't give you answers; life gives you problems to solve. The quality of your life and relationships will depend upon how well you solve those problems and your mindset through- out the process. The problems and challenges we face in relationships are bad enough, but they become un-necessarily worse when we couple those natural difficulties with the unhealthy belief these inevitable conflicts shouldn't be happening.

Look at these conflicts as relationship tests. You see a signal of a potential issue and you test the relationship to get a better understanding of the situation and make changes if necessary.

Looking at conflict as a test helps us to recognize the importance of testing *early* and *often* in relationships. You *need* to address these issues when they come up because relationships have habits just like individuals. If we don't address an issue early, we allow a potentially undesirable pattern to take hold. Like with any habit, the longer we keep that pattern, the harder it will be to change it.

For example, if you're a manager, a new member on your team might be chronically late submitting reports. The longer it takes you to say something about it, the more deeply ingrained that pattern becomes. Letting something that truly bothers you go *just because it is early in the relationship* reinforces the belief that this behavior is acceptable and makes it more likely the other party will repeat the behavior in the future. Your inaction has created negative momentum that entrenches this behavior and makes it harder to unseat.

When I hired my first administrative assistant, I led with a disclaimer. I said, "I'm going to seem really picky as we're starting off but that's because I want to make sure I let you know what I want and need as clearly as possible. This will put you in the best position to succeed." By giving this preamble to a potentially awkward conversation, I let her know my non-threatening objective *before* she had the opportunity to misinterpret the purpose and intent behind the conversation. This is an example of framing. Giving disclaimers like that helps to alleviate some of the stress the other party might feel in the conversation and opens the lines for the free flow of information.

This might be an uncomfortable approach for you because you're saying to yourself, "What if all of these relationship tests end up actually costing me the relationship?" These relationship tests have three possible outcomes:

1. You could use conflict as a tool to strengthen and improve the relationship.

2. You could use conflict as a tool to repair and maintain the relationship.

3. You could use conflict as a tool to discover that the relationship isn't worth keeping in its current state. If this is the case, you can use conflict as tool to remove or significantly alter the dynamics of the relationship.

You need to give these relationships the opportunity to fail because failure provides you with invaluable information.

If the failure results in the end of the relationship, then you just saved yourself a lot of time, energy, and future heartbreak. Without the conflict, you would've just simply delayed the inevitable and continued to invest more time and resources into a dying relationship.

We've heard the saying, "never mistake kindness for weakness," but we often fail to recognize that the opposite is also true. We should never mistake weakness for kindness.[41]

When we avoid conflict, we often convince ourselves that we're doing it out of kindness and our regard for others. The reality is that we often avoid these difficult conversations out of personal weakness and fear. It's counterintuitive, but if you care about yourself, the other person, and the relationship, the best thing to do is engage in honest conflict once you receive the signal that something is wrong.

The Alluring Trap of Intent

We've all had New Year's resolutions and we've all failed New Year's resolutions. Why? The potential reasons are endless. What matters is that there is an appreciable gap between what we said we were going to do and what we actually did.

Let's say you confidently shared a resolution with a friend, guaranteeing that you would succeed, and then you failed three weeks later. Did you just lie to the person? Were you lying to yourself?

A lie is defined as follows:

1. a false statement made with deliberate *intent* to deceive; an intentional untruth; a falsehood.[42]

2. something *intended* or serving to convey a false impression; imposture.[43]

In everyday parlance, lies and deception require intent. A lie without intent would be considered a misunderstanding or a mistake. These misunderstandings or mistakes can be done negligently or even recklessly without amounting to the same level of moral condemnation associated with lying.

Was your New Year's resolution promise a lie? Most people would say no. What if you've failed in the same way over the last ten years? *Then* was it a lie? We are privy to the running dialogue happening in our head and we have an endless amount of time to engage in introspection in order to develop a deep understanding of our motives. In spite of all this, deciphering intent *within ourselves* is still a difficult task.

How, then, can we believe that we understand the intent within the minds of others? It is an impossible task and, most importantly, an unnecessary one. You need to stay focused on the goal. The focus is on changing behavior in order to change the outcome. You can do that without interpreting intent. If you focus heavily on intent and you bring that up in the conversation, now you're having a discussion about intent, and where does that get you? Nowhere. Because it's impossible for you to know their intent and it's often difficult for them to know. So, what's the point of talking about it?

Discussing intent has the necessary effect of redirecting the focus of the conversation to the past, which is unproductive because we're not trying to change the past. We're having this conversation to collaboratively create a desirable future.

Also, when we think of these conversations in terms of intent, it impacts our performance in the conversation. Instead of focusing on problem-solving and learning in the conversation, focusing on intent naturally causes us to drift toward blaming. Blaming changes our approach to the conversation; it changes our tone and reduces our ability to be compassionate, empathetic, and curious.

This is why it's critical to fight the urge to opine on their intent. In the business world, think of it in terms of strategy, execution, outcome. People can create great strategies based on the information in front of them and execute that strategy flawlessly and still have a poor outcome. For example, if you were an investor and you did your research and you made solid investment based on the research, but you just happened to make those investments right before the recession began, you will still have a bad outcome. That doesn't denigrate that person's strategy, execution, or value as a human being.

Recognizing this reality helps us to give people the benefit of the doubt. People take offense when you question their strategy, which is linked to their intelligence and the quality of their intent. They also take offense when you question their execution, which is linked to their desire, interest, attention to detail, work ethic, and effort.

How can we approach these conversations without implicating malintent? You need to focus on the outcome and the impact. Stick to the *agreed-upon facts*. What happened? What impact did it have on you? Then steer the conversation in a productive way by orienting them to the future and turning the conversation into a joint problem-solving session where you work together to address the strategy or the execution in order to affect the outcome. This approach will lead them to feel comfortable enough to engage without being defensive.

The Benefit of the Benefit of the Doubt

We give them the benefit of the doubt for our sake more than theirs.

The benefit of the doubt can be defined as follows:

1. The belief that someone is trying the best they can given their beliefs, emotions, and current understanding of the situation.

2. Assuming the best intentions in spite of the outcomes.

I choose to give people the benefit of the doubt in difficult conversations because I want to put myself in the mindset that puts me in the best position for success. I use this when I'm serving as a mediator and I also use this when I'm negotiating with other attorneys. This might seem naïve or foolish, but it's actually the most rational thing that you can do because it leads to positive self-fulfilling prophecies and makes it easier for me to perform.

With cognitive reappraisal, we change our perception of the situation regardless of its reality. Assuming the best in others puts us in a more positive mindset. It makes us less likely to see their behavior as threatening, which keeps the amygdala at bay. This allows us to keep our prefrontal cortex engaged through- out the conversation. We give them the benefit of the doubt for our sake more than theirs.

This only works if you are keenly aware of your goals and boundaries in the discussion. As you become more skilled, you'll be able to negotiate aggressively and defend your interests without the appearance of hostility or aggression. I expect the best, but I am confident in my ability to handle the worst.

I give them the benefit of the doubt even when all signs indicate malintent from the other party. If they are behaving badly, I'm still able to keep my cool and conduct myself in a respectable fashion, which protects my reputation. I do this because I don't want to give them the excuse to behave badly because of the way I acted. Carry yourself in these conversations as if somebody that you care about and respect is watching. Would they approve of your words and actions?

Additionally, a significant amount of the underhanded tactics in difficult conversations are designed to create pressure and anxiety on you in order for you to make a mistake. They want to put you in so much emotional distress that you give in to make it stop. When you give them the benefit of the doubt, you shield yourself from the deleterious psychological effects of these tactics. You become impervious to the worst of what they can do to you.

Sometimes we learn a little bit about somebody and we paint them with a broad brush. No one is all good or all bad. In reality, we are seeing an incredibly small sample size of this person's life. If this were a study, would you have enough data points to make a conclusion? You probably need a larger sample size. Jumping to conclusions hurts your ability to persuade and connect with others.

Simply acknowledge information while withholding judgment. This helps to protect you from the alluring trap of rushing to conclusions about their intent and character. It will also protect you from creating and executing strategies that are built on flawed information.

You will give people the benefit of the doubt. You will be less hostile. And the self-fulfilling prophecy will be positive, not negative.

When people feel as though they're being accused of doing something nefarious, they are less likely to give you what you want and need. It does not move you closer to your goals. Insinuating malintent and nefarious actions is extremely risky and is problematic *even if you are correct.*

For example, if you correctly identify a liar as being a liar, they will get offended even if they were actually lying. Whether it's an accurate or inaccurate characterization, it's highly offensive when people challenge your integrity. If you've identified this person as a liar, it is more likely they would be willing to do something to hurt you in order to even the score according to their internal scales of justice.

Furthermore, you might be wrong. They might be telling the truth and their motivation might be pure. Taking this accusatory, judgmental posture limits learning. They will not feel as comfortable sharing information with you due to the increased strain on the relationship. This causes you to miss out on an opportunity to educate them and yourself because they will assume a defensive posture after the accusations.

Chapter 6

How We See the Outcomes

**We need to divorce ourselves from the
outcome and get married to the process.**

There isn't always a winner in the traditional sense, so re-
conceptualize winning. Winning is...

- Increasing understanding—of them and the
  situation.

- Sharing your story.

- Moving the needle—Rome wasn't built in a
  day.

We cannot equate worthiness with whether or not we get
what we want in these conversations. It is dangerous to
stake your self-worth on the whims of others. Don't wrap
yourself up in the outcome—have you ever tried to negotiate with a two- year-old?

It also helps me make the whole thing less personal. No
matter what I do and how good I perform, I know I could
do everything perfectly and still not get what I want just

because of the perspective or behavior of the other side. If this breaks down, but I do things right, it's not on me and I can feel comfortable with the outcome. I'm not as focused on the outcome as I am on the process and, more so, my goal is not necessarily outcome-oriented as much as it is process-oriented.

Likewise, my goal is not a specific outcome; my goal is a specific feeling, which is peace. Am I at peace with my performance? Am I improving? If I am at peace with my performance, I know I did the best that I could. Regardless of the outcome, I can rest assured that I put myself in the best position for success. In my negotiation philosophy, knowing that the outcome clearly wasn't for me allows me to be at peace even though I am disappointed. I believe enough in myself that another one will come along.

One of the craziest things about conflict is that not every conflict needs to have a solution. Not every conflict ends in agreement. The goal of a conflict agreement is understanding. Once you reach understanding, if an agreement exists, it will be a lot easier to find.

Negotiation isn't the art of deal making; it is the art of deal discovery. You work with the other side in order to determine whether or not the deal exists. We should approach conflict in the same way. We ask questions in order to learn more and work with them in order to determine whether or not a resolution exists.

After every difficult conversation, ask yourself what benefit you gained from having that conversation. This is especially important for people who struggle with difficult conversations because you need to see value. You need to see some return on the emotional investment of the conversation. This will also help to solidify the habit because, in order for a habit to stick, there needs to be a reward and that reward needs to come reasonably soon after the behavior.

There is a difference between a defeat and a strategic retreat.

Whenever you find yourself in this situation, ask yourself, "Am I putting myself in the best position for success?"

Primary vs. Secondary Goals

In a salary negotiation, your ultimate goal is to get more money. If that negotiation doesn't result in a better compensation package, was the negotiation a failure? It's easy to feel that way if we have an unhealthy and narrow perspective of success and failure in these difficult conversations.

In these conversations, there are going to be primary goals and secondary goals. The primary goal in every conversation should be the same—improve your skills, abilities, and confidence in difficult conversations. This is a goal you can accomplish *every time* you perform. Even if you didn't get what you wanted in your secondary goal, you're still winning as long as you're improving.

This mindset of continuous improvement helps us to be more process-oriented than outcome-oriented in these difficult conversations. Focusing on the process is what leads to the true development of skills and long-term growth. You will be more threatened by failure if you have a short-term definition of a win or a loss.

On its face, it might seem odd to prioritize this over the substantive outcome. However, the reality is that focusing on the process results in putting ourselves in the best possible position to get what we want because we engage the process more effectively.

Physical fitness is a fun challenge for me because it is the pursuit of perfection with the healthy understanding that perfection is an unattainable goal. There is always something you can do to improve yourself physically. Similarly, there is always something we can do to improve ourselves with regard to our performance in difficult conversations.

When you consider your improvement in this realm, you should focus on improving in three key categories—mindset, strategy, and execution. With all my negotiation seminars, I encourage people to do a "post-game analysis" of every conversation and I give them an outline for how to do it. This structured analysis will help you to think about these conversations more strategically and will lead to rapid improvement. This is because you'll be able to actually pinpoint what you did well, what you did poorly, and what you can do to better next time.

Chess.com has a chat function that is used solely for the purpose of talking trash to your opponents. One time in law school I was in a heated series of games with a player from the United Kingdom. I was gloating after I won a game. Then my opponent said something that I'll never forget: "I'm 12."

I sat there, mouth agape, then responded with my only possible comeback. I said, "I'm 11." Then I left.

How is it possible I was struggling to beat a 12-year old after thousands of games of chess? It's because I just play for fun. I play to pass the time and I play with friends for bragging rights. I don't practice my skills or read books on it or practice isolated parts of the game in order to get a better understanding of it. As a result, my skills have, predictably, plateaued. Without deliberate, intentional, targeted practice of your negotiation and conflict management skills, your abilities will inevitably begin to stagnate, too.

It's troubling how much money is left on the table simply because professionals who are negotiating six and seven-figure deals for their companies enter the process without the skills necessary to get the best deals. Many haven't received negotiation trainings that teach the fundamentals of psychology in conjunction with customized negotiation simulations.

This is why it's so important to have the opportunity to practice deliberately and intentionally through rigorous training programs. Even if you are somebody who negotiates every day, if you haven't practiced intentionally, you might just be a 20- year novice or a recreational negotiator, not an expert negotiator.

The License to Fail

Your goal isn't to be perfect, your goal is to be better than yesterday.

You have the license to fail when it comes to your secondary goal, but you don't have a license to fail when it comes to your primary goal because whether or not you improve is completely within your grasp.

The license to fail is the antidote to perfectionism. When we believe in perfection or seek perfection, we won't act until we think we can win or deliver the perfect performance. There will always be a reason why perfection is unattainable and, as a result, there are many reasons why we decide not to engage. Fear feeds on time and the longer we try to find the perfect way to approach the conversation, the more fearful we will become.

The license to fail allows you to pursue perfection with the understanding that there is no such thing. It is a constant journey toward mastery. You will make mistakes; they are part of the process. In fact, mistakes should be celebrated because they show that you are trying. You are giving yourself the opportunity to fail, which means you're pushing yourself. If all you do is "win win win no matter what," it's a sign that you're not trying very hard. This is why giving people the license to fail is so liberating. Your goal isn't to be perfect; your goal is to be better than yesterday.

You will gain confidence from knowing that you *will* fail in some capacity in each and every one of these conversations and you will *still* have the skills to survive and thrive on the other side. The things that used to scare you will still scare you, but you will learn to see these scary stimuli as opportunities.

This approach gives you more power than resilience. Resilience is withstanding difficult circumstances and staying the same. Resilience is admirable, but evolution is superior. Human advancement and evolution are predicated upon encountering difficult circumstances and not just surviving but finding ways to thrive. Conflict is an opportunity for evolution. Win, lose, or draw, you should come out on the other side better in some way. The best things in life lie on the other side of difficult conversations. If you are able to evolve, you will avail yourself to the spoils that come with the best things in life.

This mindset allows you to win in spite of failure. If you take chances and engage in these difficult conversations, you might not get the specific outcome you're looking for, but regardless you are winning because you are evolving. You are better now after the conversation than you were before the conversation because you are improving your skills. Failure isn't a loss unless you fail to learn in the process.

I've read about the benefits of meditation for years. Every time I tried to incorporate the practice into my life, I would fail because I got frustrated. It seemed unattainable. I would try to think of nothing, but I only succeeded in thinking of everything. Am I broken? Are all these "zen" people faking it? What's wrong with me?

All of that changed when I downloaded the Headspace application on my phone. Headspace is an application with hundreds of guided meditations. One of the reasons why I like the Headspace app is because Andy, the person who guides you, doesn't focus on "the perfect meditation" where your mind is completely clear. He lets you know that your mind will wander and that's OK. This was groundbreaking. Telling me that imperfection is acceptable was incredibly encouraging.

This slight mental shift made all the difference in my practice of meditation. My goal became improvement, not perfection. Now meditation is an integral part of my mental strength training regimen. It has helped me to be more self-aware in difficult conversations and in my everyday life. I've been able to develop the habit of meditation by recognizing the importance of consistent, *imperfect* action. In other words, having the license to fail was the key to my success.

The license to fail is a gift you give yourself that liberates you from the tyranny of perfection. In order to find confidence in conflict, you need to develop a habit of engagement. The only way you can develop this habit is through consistent action. However, you won't take action if you're striving for perfection or paralyzed by the fear of failure.

As you start to develop the habit of engagement, you will try new techniques and approaches and you will fail at times. Look at that failure as information, a brand-new data point for you to consider. Think of yourself as a curious scientist and these conversations are your experiments. "Well, that certainly didn't work. Why didn't it work? What could I have done differently?" The license to fail is really the license to try. If you're doing it right, your confidence will grow in success and in failure.

Mastery isn't necessarily about being the best at something; it is about a process. It is about progress and learning to develop an appetite for the challenge. The byproduct of mastery is confidence.

Gender

If you tell a lion she's a kitten enough times, she'll believe you.

Disclaimer: For those of you who don't know, I am a man.

As an aspiring feminist[44], I am not blind to the unavoidable patriarchy in play as a man opining about women in negotiation. I strive to be an ally and that's why I am honored to serve on the national board of Women for Economic and Leadership Development. Based on the questions I regularly receive on the topic of gender dynamics in negotiation, I would be remiss to overlook such an important issue in this book.

That's also why Katherine Knapke, our Chief Operating Officer, hosts the Ask With Confidence Podcast, which is a show for women by women on the topic of negotiation. This free resource is a treasure trove of valuable insights about gender dynamics and much more.

Now we can begin.

I was presenting at a conference for a chapter of the National Association of Women Business Owners and one of the women in the audience asked me, "How do you stand up for yourself if you are a bad negotiator?"

I responded by saying, "First, I'd like to offer a minor revision to the way that you asked the question. You should have said, 'How do you stand up for yourself if you're not a great negotiator *yet*?' This is because negotiation and conflict management are skills, not talents. They can be learned."

She mentioned earlier in the presentation that she had children, so I asked, "If somebody was mistreating your child, would you be able to stand up for her?"

She said, "Of course!"

Then I said, "So it's not a situation where you don't know how to stand up and be assertive. The reality is that you don't know how to stand up and be assertive *for yourself*."

Then I posed this question to the women in the audience: "What kind of games did you play when you were growing up?"

The majority of them said they played with Barbies and played house.

Then I asked the three men in the audience what kind of games they played in their youth. They said they played sports or games like tag.

When I asked the women what the goal was for their games, they said they were all social goals like keeping a good house, getting married, maintaining relationships, etc. Then I asked the guys what the goal was for their games and they said, "To win!" To emphasize the point, I asked the guys, "What happens if you win the game and somebody on the other team starts crying?" The guys in the audience sat in silence for a little bit but they all had this slight smirk on their faces and then finally one of them said, "That's awesome!" And I said, "Right!? That's bonus points!"

The goals for the games little girls play are focused on social cohesion and the games that little boys play are focused on competitiveness. Over the course of your childhood, those types of stereotypes are constantly reinforced and it molds the way you think about social interactions. Often when girls try to cross over and play those stereotypically male games, a well-meaning teacher or parent says, "No, no, those games are for boys. Little girls do this..." Similarly, in group activities when a boy takes the role of leader, he is called assertive, which has a positive connotation. However, if a girl takes the role of leader, she is called bossy, which carries a negative connotation. Thus, when a little girl tries to be competitive, assume a leadership position, or stand up for herself, she is constantly told, either implicitly or explicitly, that it is inappropriate.

However, there is a catch. Even though women are taught throughout their lives not to assert themselves on behalf of themselves, they are taught that it is OK to assert themselves on behalf of others. Some refer to this as the "mama bear" mentality. The mama bear will protect her cubs. Interestingly, this mentality expands to other people or entities under their watch as well. Thus, a woman might be able to negotiate effectively on behalf of her company or her clients if she is an attorney but, at the same time, may find it difficult to negotiate on her own behalf for a higher salary or to advance on the partnership track.

What can we do about this? When I'm coaching female executives who struggle in this area, I focus first on addressing their mindset and how they think of themselves. If they think of themselves as themselves, they struggle. However, if they imagine they are playing the role of someone else, they thrive.[45]

For example, for the woman who asked the question at the presentation, I said, "It's clear that as a mother you don't have any issue standing up for your children. From now on, before every difficult conversation, I want you to ask yourself, 'if my daughter were in my current position and I were advocating on her behalf, how would I act? What would I say? How assertive would I be?'"

For those of you who aren't mothers, you could ask yourself, "If I were an attorney tasked with representing someone in my current position, how would I act? What would I say? How assertive would I be?"

Playing this type of mental perspective-changing game can help you find the right tone and the right words in these difficult conversations. This approach is especially powerful for women who are able to stand up for others but struggle to stand up for themselves. If they can see themselves as someone else through this exercise, they'll feel more comfortable advocating on their own behalf.

Often times we struggle to stand up for ourselves because we put the needs of others in front of our own. Interestingly, we can even put the needs of the opposing party in front of our needs. We are afraid of making the other side feel uncomfortable.

Women tend to be especially sensitive to this because, as dis- cussed earlier, women have been socialized to focus on social cohesion over self-focused competitiveness. Additionally, women experience more social judgment than men.

This is a competitive world and, in the business world especially, you can't depend on other people to keep your best interests at heart. You need to assume that you will be your best advocate and that if you aren't standing up for yourself, no one else will.

I was recently invited to speak at the Women Lawyers of Franklin County luncheon. Someone made the comment that it often feels as though the cards are stacked against her. She's a young, female, minority attorney who happens to be 5'1". There seems to be a significant power discrepancy when opposing counsel is a 6'2" white male the age of her grandfather.

The Compassionate Curiosity Framework provides a solution for this situation when used *internally*.

1. Acknowledge Emotion: In this situation, she feels as though there's an advantage on the other side.

2. Compassionate Curiosity: Why do I feel this way? Where is this feeling coming from?

3. Joint Problem-Solving: What is a solution that is acceptable to both my heart and mind?

In this case, we'll spend the majority of our time in the curiosity stage. Here, it's important to learn to distinguish between objective advantage and perceived advantage. The power advantage is legitimate if they have some tangible leverage over you. There are three sources of this leverage—positive, negative, and normative.

- Positive leverage: they have something you want.

- Negative leverage: they can do something that you don't want them to do to hurt you (or your client)

- Normative leverage: the rule of law or the unwritten rules of society are in their favor.[46]

Is there a true power advantage? If the answer is no, then the pressure you're feeling is coming from your own mind and may be amplified by the gamesmanship of the other side. This is a red herring and should be ignored.

Interestingly, for women, advocating for themselves at home may be one of the most important types of difficult conversations for working women. In dual-income homes with heterosexual partners, women do a disproportionate amount of the domestic work. In these kinds of relationships, women typically do around 33 hours of work at home per week while men typically do between 14 and 18 hours of work at home. This explains why stress levels for women often *increase* when the work day ends. This helps to explain why the amount of depression in working women is significantly higher than men, too.[47] In these scenarios, effective negotiation with a partner may lead to a significant improvement in mental health.

Conclusion

This is a brand-new approach to difficult conversations. It's going to take some time for you to find your feet and make it your own, but it won't happen if you sit and think about it. Adopting these mindsets will liberate you from the behavior of others dictating your emotional status. If you constantly allow people to dictate your emotions and the quality of your ability to perform, you are giving them a disproportionate amount of power in your life. This new mindset will give you the control you're looking for. Create your own emotional reality.

These thoughtful responses to difficult conversations are un- natural and often unpleasant. Because of that, it will take a lot of mental and emotional energy to perform well in these conversations. Think of every conversation you have as a training opportunity. Every day, you are training for the bigger conversations, the ones that matter. When the time comes for these critical conversations, you are ready because you have been spending all of this time practicing, training, preparing, etc., and you have the mental and emotional energy necessary to perform at a high level.

Chapter 7

Understanding and Building Confidence

Confidence can be defined as follows:

1. Confidence is a feeling of self-assurance that comes from an appreciation of your abilities.[48]

2. Confidence is a feeling that you can rely on someone or something in order to affect an outcome.[49]

Confidence is an attitude that affects the way that you navigate the world. One of the most interesting things about confidence is that it can be compartmentalized. You can be supremely confident when it comes to the specifics of your profession and completely lacking in confidence when it comes to having difficult conversations within your profession.[50]

When I surveyed my podcast listeners to see their main challenges in difficult conversations, confidence was one of their top concerns. You're not alone in this.

People often ask me how I *act* confident in negotiations. The problem with this question is that you're starting in the wrong place.

If you plant an acorn what will you get? You'll get an oak tree. We are not surprised that specific seeds will lead to the germination and growth of specific plants. Thus, how you carry yourself in negotiations is simply a manifestation of what's inside. If you are truly confident, that confidence will naturally blossom into confident body language.

People make the mistake of focusing exclusively on what can be seen: behavior. "Don't sit like that. Don't talk like that. Raise your chin. Straighten your back, etc." Although this advice is well-intentioned, it overlooks the fact that these unpersuasive words and behaviors stem from your lack of confidence.

Actors receive specialized instruction to change their behaviors and the way they carry themselves in order to play a specific role. I'm assuming that you haven't received this kind of training. Neither have I. Thus, it's safe to assume that we can't act well enough to persuade the people around us in these difficult conversations.

You won't be able to convince them *with* your abilities if you are not convinced *of* your abilities. When you try to simply adjust your behavior without adjusting your beliefs or mindset, you're essentially becoming a bad actor. You're trying to embody the movements and language that demonstrate confidence in spite of its absence.

When your body and mind are out of sync, it produces something called asynchronous behavior. This is often seen as a time lag between your thoughts and actions or a lack of symmetry between beliefs and behaviors.[51] For example, if your four-year old nephew decides to cook for you and asks if you like the food, you might take a few extra seconds to respond, then you might subtly shake your head no while saying yes.

This occurs because you have a thought and then, instead of responding with an action that is in line with your true belief, you edit your behavior. You don't need to be a body language expert to pick up on this. The person on the receiving end will notice the asynchrony, but they won't know exactly what it is. It will come off as inauthenticity at best and deception at worst, both of which are contrary to relationship-building and persuasion.

There is a big difference between trying to *act* confident and actually *being* confident. Therefore, the keys to becoming a confident communicator are to

1. Discover the genesis of your lack of confidence (introspection), and

2. Remedy your lack of confidence in order to lead to lasting behavioral changes by changing your mindset and improving your skills.

What Are the Benefits of Confidence?

**If you sound convinced,
you're more likely to be convincing.**

Confidence Leads to Opportunity

Have you ever looked at someone who's successful or high-ranking and thought to yourself, "I could do that. In fact, I could probably do what they're doing *better* than them. But if that's true, why are they there and why am I here?" This happens, in large part, due to three main reasons:

1. They know people.

2. They asked those people for what they want.

3. They sounded confident when they asked for it.

The first point is all about networking and connections. The more people you know, the more *potential* opportunities will come your way. I emphasize the word potential because simply being privy to these opportunities is not enough. It requires action and persuasion to take advantage of them.

Let's look at the second point on the list. It's not enough to know what you want; you need to take the steps to acquire it. The first step in any negotiation is the ask. Most of us lose before we even begin because we don't ask for what we want.

One of the best books on the gender dynamics in negotiation is called *Women Don't Ask* by Linda Babcock and Sara Laschever. The central premise of the book is that a significant portion of the discrepancy in negotiation outcomes between men and women originates from the reality that men are simply more likely to ask for what they want.[52]

To the third point, if you sound convinced, you're more likely to be convincing. Before you negotiate with the other person, you need to address the *internal* negotiation that occurs with- in the confines of your own mind. This is where confidence, preparation, and ability come into play. Do you believe you? If the answer is no, then neither will they. You need to have confidence in the substance of your argument and in your capacity to convey it.

Confidence Leads to Committed Action

Confidence is the purity of action produced by a mind free of unhealthy worry or doubt.[53] The more confidence you have, the more likely you are to take action toward your goal and the more likely you are to convey your wants and needs in a persuasive manner.

Think about a time when you had to make an important choice but you were crippled with indecision. How did you feel? What stopped you from making a decision and taking committed action? Indecision often results from a cacophony of reasons, arguments, and fears that rage around your head like a hurricane. You conceive a series of "what ifs," each more terrifying than the last, that paralyze you and constrain your ability to act.

Interestingly, studies suggest that the topics of confidence and action may be impacted by gender. According to Katy Kay and Claire Shipman in *The Confidence Code*:

"Remember, the female brain works differently from the male brain; we really do have more going on, we are more keenly aware of everything happening around us, and that all becomes part of our cognitive stew. Ruminating drains the confidence from us."[54]

In part three of the book, I will provide you with a framework for handling the most difficult internal and external conflicts of your life. One of the benefits of a framework is that it doesn't only tell you what you need to focus on; it also tells you what you need to ignore. This framework will help to clear your mind and empower you to take committed action toward your goals.

Confidence Improves Performance

Effective persuasion requires two parties. There is the party delivering the message and the party receiving the message. What's fascinating is that the confidence of one party has a profound impact on both parties. Numerous studies have shown that individuals who sound confident and individuals who can carry themselves with authority are considered to be more persuasive by the other side.

When it comes to practice and professional development, sports has always been on the cutting edge. An example of this can be seen in the sports psychology industry. Almost every major professional sports team has one of these professionals on its roster.

Sports psychology is rooted in the belief that mental and emotional strength are critical to performance. According to sports psychologists, confidence can be the difference between success and failure in professional sports.

Confidence can impact the way we see the world. Golfers with more confidence perceive the hole to be bigger, which increases their belief in their ability to guide the ball into the hole. Tennis players with more confidence perceive the ball to be bigger, which increases their belief in their ability to hit the ball cleanly. Has the realty changed? No. Their confidence impact- ed their perception and as a result of that new perception, there is improved performance.[55]

How would the world look to you if you saw these difficult conversations as more manageable and the goals on the other side as more achievable? You'll be more likely to engage whole- heartedly and take committed action because you can finally see the potential for success. That alone will lead to improved performance in these difficult conversations.

Confidence not only has a positive impact on your performance, but it also impacts the way others see you. Numerous studies have demonstrated that people are more likely to be persuaded by those they *perceive* as having authority. For example, in Cialdini's landmark book, *Influence*, he named authority as one of the six key mental shortcuts that influence decision-making and lead to persuasion.[56]

A key part of the persuasive power of authority is the reality that simply *being* an authority figure isn't enough. They've found that you also need to carry yourself as someone with authority. This is where confidence comes into play.

For example, having the title of an attorney carries some level of authority by itself. However, if that attorney speaks with trepidation, hesitation, and uncertainty, they lose a significant portion of the persuasive power that comes with their profession.

Authority can be incredibly narrow. For example, if you prepare thoroughly and carry yourself as an authority on the nuances of *this specific deal or conflict*, you can reap the persuasive benefits that come with being seen as an authority. Competence breeds confidence. The more thoroughly you prepare, the more confident you will be and the more authority you will wield.

The landmark experiment in authority was done by Stanley Milgram.[57] The participants in the study were led into a room where they were greeted by a man wearing a white lab coat. They were told that there was an individual in another room, referred to as the "learner," who was going to be quizzed. The role of the participants was to administer incrementally increasing levels of electric shocks to the learner when he got the questions wrong. What they didn't know was that the learner wasn't a real person, it was just a recording.

As the shocks became more intense, so did the recorded cries for help from the other side. The learner would plead to be released, he would complain of a heart condition, and he would scream. The discomfort of the participants rose with the severity of the shocks and the intensity of the screams. The participants would beg to stop, but the man in the white lab coat who was "running the experiment" confidently told them to continue.

At the end of the experiment 65% of the participants punished the learner with a potentially life-threatening amount of electric shock and 100% administered up to a severe level of shock.

Why did they do this? Because the person was wearing a white lab coat, which signified authority, and the person who made the request sounded confident and authoritative. When you put those things together, there was compliance. We give confidence an inordinate amount of weight when it comes to persuasion.[58]

How to Gain Confidence

The Positive Cycle of Confidence

One of the seemingly magical qualities of confidence is the fact that it makes you more likely to take action. It is a self-perpetuating phenomenon where confidence leads you to take more action, action leads to positive results, and the results make you more confident. This makes you more likely to take action in the future. Thus, confidence results in action and also grows *as a result of* that action.

This is where the quote "fake it till you make it" comes into play. You don't just wait for your confidence to grow; you need to force yourself to take action in order for it to grow. We need to develop the habit of engagement.

Whenever you see an opportunity to engage in a difficult conversation, you need to take advantage of it. We often make the mistake of seeing these simply as opportunities to get what we want, avoid things we don't want, and strengthen our relationships. However, learning to see these difficult conversations as an opportunity to grow our confidence and improve our skills is just as important as the results of these conversations.

The effects of confidence compound. If you are decisive and take committed action, it will give you more confidence for the next difficult conversation. This will make you more likely to take action the next time and it will keep getting easier and easier.

People often make the mistake of conflating confidence with comfort. They think that their discomfort is a sign that they shouldn't take action, or they take it as an indictment of their abilities. You need to learn how to push through that initial discomfort in spite of your feelings. Developing the habits of thorough preparation and committed action are the best ways to improve your confidence.

Why the Action-Oriented Approach Works

"Do one thing every day that scares you."
Eleanor Roosevelt

One of my favorite TED Talks is called *What I Learned from 100 Days of Rejection* by Jia Jiang,[59] where he chronicles his fascinating journey to overcome the fear of rejection and failure. His strategy was to intentionally seek rejection for 100 days in order to desensitize himself from its painful sting. Some of his requests were simple and mundane and some were more elaborate. His discoveries fall perfectly in line with gaining confidence in conflict:

1. He discovered that there is life after rejection. The world didn't end. His family and friends still loved him. After he felt the rejection, he just moved on to the next one. The list of horrors that our worried mind can contrive often don't come to pass.

2. He discovered that a no can become a yes. **We often make the mistake of conflating rejection and resistance.** The only way you can distinguish between the two is through persistence.

3. He discovered that a number of requests he thought were impossible were actually attainable. As he progressed, his requests became more ex-

124

treme. For example, one time he went to a donut shop and asked for them to make him some donuts in the shape and colors of the Olympic rings. And he got it! This begs the question, what in life have we missed out on simply because we failed to ask?

These findings were critical for me on my own personal journey from people-pleaser to confident negotiator. I began not only to engage in rejection therapy, but to also intentionally put myself in uncomfortable situations because I knew it would make me stronger over time.

I used to work at a nonprofit that provided federally funded job opportunities and professional development to low-income young adults. In order to qualify for the program, you needed to pass an interview and meet specific income eligibility requirements. For example, if an individual came from a household with four people, the household income couldn't be more than $50,200. If that household brought in $50,200.01, they would be ineligible for the program.

This resulted in the heart-wrenching situation where, although someone was poor, they were not poor enough to take advantage of this life-changing opportunity. Telling the families that they earned "too much money" to participate in the program was devastating to me and my colleagues at the program and we all dreaded those conversations.

After watching Jia Jiang's TED Talk, I decided that I would take this as an opportunity to expose myself to my fears. I told my colleagues that I would make all the calls to the families who didn't qualify to let them know they couldn't participate. I volunteered to break their hearts.

As a people-pleaser, this was worse than physical pain. A little part of me died every time I sat down in front of them and saw the excitement in their eyes turn to frustration, disappointment, and anger.

However, when my time at the program came to a close, I realized something. The little part of me that died every time was weakness. Every time I forced myself to have these difficult conversations, I pruned a part of myself that held me back. I started to feel liberated and empowered. I had these difficult conversations and I survived. I could finally say what I knew I needed to say *in spite* of the fear, and this realization helped reduce the power fear held over me.

To this day, those were some of the most difficult conversations I've had, and I still look back on that experience for strength

Today, difficult conversations are much easier for me. However, I still feel fear, discomfort, and trepidation when they arise. The difference is that now I have the confidence to push through those emotions in order to have the difficult conversations that I worked so hard to avoid in the past. I use my fear as a signal to approach, not avoid.

With rejection therapy, we are essentially treating our fear of difficult conversations and rejection as a low-grade mental illness. We are taking advantage of everyday opportunities to engage in difficult conversations and ask for what we want in order to overcome the fear and anxiety we've been feeling. This is something I *still* do as an attorney in order to keep my skills sharp.

This explains why role-playing activities are a critical part of my trainings when I travel the country teaching professionals about negotiation and conflict management. However, since I'm not there with you, we're going to have to use the honor system. In order for you to increase your confidence in these difficult conversations and maximize the value of the frame- work, you need to commit to take action. Commit to engaging in rejection therapy and see your confidence soar. Eventually you will dull the fear enough to allow you to take action more consistently.

One trick you can use to increase the likelihood of taking committed action is to create an action equation. Make the following promise: "I'll take action if..." This allows you to decide whether or not you should engage or let it go *before* it's time to take action. *If* those criteria are met, *then* you'll engage in the difficult conversation.

Here's an example. Let's say you're a business owner and you have a partner. You and your partner decided to have weekly meetings to discuss what's going right, what's going wrong, and what changes need to be made in the business. The problem is that last week your partner cancelled the meeting at the last minute and this week they showed up late and seemed to be disengaged. You determine that these two instances may be outliers and you're willing to let it slide. However, *if* they cancel or seem disengaged again within the next six weeks, *then* you'll have a serious conversation with them within 48 hours of the incident to discuss the situation.

Also take inventory of your best excuses. We often have preferred excuses that we allow to stand in the way of taking action. Write them down and familiarize yourself with them so you can recognize them as illegitimate excuses when they arise.

What's happening here is that we come to our preferred conclusions automatically based on our feelings and emotions. We then subsequently explain how we arrived at these conclusions through rationalizations that take the form of excuses and feed these excuses to ourselves and others to justify our choices.

Expanding on the example above, let's say that you, as the business owner, are deathly afraid of conflict. That's your ingrained emotional response to the prospect of difficult conversations. Thus, your preferred conclusion leads you to avoid difficult conversations. You may then rationalize your decision to avoid the conversation by saying to yourself, "I shouldn't have this conversation because...

- I don't want to ruin team chemistry."

- They might get mad and leave the business."

- Nothing bad really happened as a result of their absence."

- I'm lucky to have them."

- I'm horrible in these conversations and I'll just make things worse."

- It's not that big of a deal.

Remember, giving people the benefit of the doubt doesn't mean that you allow them to take advantage of you. You need to combat these logical fallacies systematically. Identify the thought and test its legitimacy. If, upon further analysis, you determine that it's illegitimate, then you cannot let it be a barrier to engaging in these conversations. We'll explore this further when we address how to handle negotiations with yourself.

We're creating a new habit. In the past, the habit was the *trigger* of negative emotions and an unpleasant physiological response, the *behavior* of running away or avoiding the conflict or not engaging in it the right way, and the *benefit* of not having a conflict anymore. That was your reward. Now it's going to be the same trigger, the negative emotional response or physiological response, a new behavior, which is to move toward it, and a new reward, which is better relationships and better negotiation outcomes.

Self-Compassion and Self-Forgiveness

Treat yourself like you would a doubles partner.

I've been playing tennis since age five and it's by far my favorite sport. For the purposes of this section, all I need you to know is that in tennis you can either play singles (by yourself against another person) or doubles (with a partner against an- other pair).

Mistakes are inevitable in tennis, and when you play doubles it won't always be you making the mistakes. Here's what's fascinating: in all of my years of playing tennis, I've never seen a doubles player verbally abuse or chastise a partner (unless they are playing with a sibling). The communication between the teammates is typically limited to strategy, encouragement, and forgiveness. However, self-directed verbal abuse abounds when people play singles. Why? It's a lot easier to be compassionate and forgiving to your friends than it is to be compassionate and forgiving to yourself.

Some of the best advice I've heard when it comes to tennis is to treat yourself like a doubles partner. You are often your own worst critic. You need to treat yourself with the same empathy, respect, compassion, and forgiveness you would give to a teammate. Players almost always give their doubles partner the benefit of the doubt and tacitly assume that their partner is trying the best they can under the circumstances. We need to do the same for ourselves.

Self-forgiveness is about repairing the emotional damage you've done to yourself. The goal is to "resolve guilt, shame, disappointment and other emotions that arise when you see a discrepancy between what you believe in and something you've done."[60] You've beaten yourself up and now you're healing yourself.

According to Dr. Kristen Neff, there are three elements of self-compassion[61]:

1. Self-kindness vs. Self-judgment: You need to treat yourself with warmth and understanding when you suffer, fail, or feel inadequate, rather than ignoring your pain or flagellating yourself with self-criticism.

2. Common Humanity vs. Isolation: You need to recognize that suffering and personal inadequacy

are part of the shared human experience. The suffering that comes with fear, anxiety, and failure often is combined with a feeling of isolation. You feel like this is unique to you. It's liberating to know that these feelings are shared by billions of people around the world. You're not a failure. You're not broken. You're human.

3. Mindfulness vs. Over-identification: Self-compassion also requires taking a balanced approach to our negative emotions so that feelings are neither suppressed nor exaggerated. You must be willing to observe your negative thoughts and emotions with openness and clarity so that they are held in mindful awareness.

Self-forgiveness and self-compassion are going to be critical as you embark on this journey because failure is a necessary part of the process. It's especially important if you suffer from unhealthy competitiveness or perfectionism.

People often believe that they need to be hard on themselves in order improve and progress. In reality, self-compassion is the tool that allows you to take risks. This is because you know that you won't beat yourself up and make yourself feel worse after the potential failure. Constant self-criticism brings you down, which puts you in an unhealthy mental state and prevents you from taking committed action.

I cannot emphasize this point enough. As you start to build a habit of engaging in difficult conversations, it is going to hurt. It's going to be awkward and uncomfortable, and many times it will not go well. Those unpleasant and uncomfortable feelings and those repeated failures are a necessary part of the process. This is why self-forgiveness and self-compassion are so critical. These tools are the fundamental elements of true resilience. Before, you may have let those feelings steer you away from conflict or inhibit your performance. However, if you use self-forgiveness and self-compassion, those same feelings will inspire you because it means that you're moving in the right direction.

Self-forgiveness and self-compassion are the unsung heroes of self-confidence. On the front end, they reduce your paralyzing fear and anxiety because you know that your internal voice won't be overly critical. They also give you the resilience you need to come back stronger if you do fail.

I've found that my confidence, assertiveness, and willingness to take committed action comes in large part due to my mindset. The way we see these difficult conversations will have a significant impact on how we perform. We'll discuss this more in the next chapter.

In order to build this new habit of engagement we must protect the habit. We've all tried New Year's resolutions and we have all failed at New Year's. resolutions. Why? This explanation applies not only to New Year's resolutions but also habit creation in general. One of the reasons we fail is because we envision ourselves performing this new habit in perfect circumstances. I'm going to wake up, I'm going to put on my clothes, and I'm going to go to the gym at 5:30 a.m. But rarely do these new habits happen in a vacuum. Life happens, and life is messy and unpredictable. We need to protect these habits from life getting in the way. The excuses for poor performance will always outnumber the reasons for high-level performance. However, even though the reasons are outnumbered, they should not be outweighed. In order to protect this habit, we need to try to envision the type of resistance we will face. What are the things that will get in the way and interfere with this habit? Then we need to come up with strategies to deal with those situations.

Chapter 8

THE COMPASSIONATE CURIOSITY FRAMEWORK

There's a difference between effective communication and persuasive communication.

If I were to sum up the benefit of this book in one word it would be control. We are allowing the world to shape us every time we choose *not* to engage in these difficult conversations. Being proactive about engaging in these conversations gives us a unique opportunity to take control of the most significant parts of our lives; our business and personal relationships.

When you get to a certain level in your career, competence is assumed. What will truly be the differentiating factor is your ability to interact with others, especially under pressure. This is one of the quintessential elements of leadership.

Effective communication isn't enough to get you where you want to go. With effective communication the other side understands your perspective and you understand theirs. The problem is that you may clearly communicate your wants and needs to the other side and they may clearly understand; however, they still ultimately may not be moved to change their positions or behaviors. With persuasive communication you are blending efficacy *and* persuasiveness. Not only do they understand what you want but then they agree and act accordingly. That's what we really want out of these difficult conversations.

Why are you reading this book? You're reading this because you care about something. You have goals, hopes, and dreams and you recognize something is holding you back. The quality of your relationships and the amount of success and failure you experience in your career will be determined in large part by the way you perform in these difficult conversations.

You're most likely not only doing this for yourself, you're also doing it for the people who depend on you - your family, your coworkers, your clients, etc. You're not just trying to communicate effectively, you're trying to inspire change for a specific purpose.

After you learn how to use the Compassionate Curiosity Framework you will know what to say and how to say it in your most difficult conversations. This is a technique I've used throughout my career as a business lawyer and a mediator. I also use it every day as a husband, father, and friend.

We have two lives: the life we live and the life we are capable of living. Don't let poor performance in these difficult conversations hold you back from what you want, need, and deserve. You know where you want to go; let The Compassionate Curiosity Framework show you how to get there.[62]

The Framework

The steps for the Compassionate Curiosity Framework are simple:

1. Acknowledge Emotion.

2. Compassionate Curiosity.

3. Joint Problem-Solving.

This approach is designed to be simple enough for you to remember in the midst of your most difficult conversations. Even if you just remember the term, you'll improve your ability to perform in the conversation.

You need to ask yourself, "What does Compassionate Curiosity mean to me?" Take this framework and make it your own. You will struggle if you become rigid and dogmatic with the approach. It needs to be organic, it needs to flow, and it needs to be in line with your natural way of interacting with others.

Compassionate Curiosity is simply my attempt to articulate my process of handling difficult conversations based on my experience as a mediator, attorney, and negotiation trainer. Do I go through this in a regimented fashion? No. However, Compassionate Curiosity is a systematic approach to negotiation that makes room for the requisite flexibility to be able to move nimbly within a difficult conversation. This approach helps me make sure I never get lost in these conversations.

Compassionate Curiosity puts you in the best position for success in difficult conversations; however, it comes with an additional benefit. Using this model will make you a better conversationalist in general. It will make you a more generous conversational partner and people will want to talk and share more with you. I can't tell you how many times someone has started a sentence in with, "Kwame, I've never told anybody this, but..." It is no longer surprising to me when this happens—even *if it's our first conversation*. Why does this happen? Using Compassionate Curiosity inspires trust. They feel comfortable with me and they trust that they can be vulnerable because they don't believe I will take advantage of them.

One of the reasons we don't engage in difficult conversations is because of the ambiguity or apparent chaos within them. Uncertainty is uncomfortable.

This is actually one of the things that leads to procrastination. You don't know what to do first, so you just don't do anything. In many productivity books, they suggest breaking down tasks into a step-by-step process so you know what to do first. That is what we are doing with this process of Compassionate Curiosity. We are disambiguating the process by providing a simple, systematic approach.

People often feel overwhelmed in difficult conversations because of superfluous externalities, which is a fancy way of saying that we pay attention to things that are not important. Experts don't only know what to focus on; they also know what to ignore.

This framework brings order to chaos. No matter how complex and how messy the conversation gets, you will be able to know where you are, what you need to do, and what you need to say.

Finally, Compassionate Curiosity is designed to help you to master both internal and external negotiation. It will help you gain a greater level of control over your own psychology as well as the psychology of the other side.

INTERNAL USAGE OF COMPASSIONATE CURIOSITY

Before we master these conversations we must first master ourselves.

Several departments are involved when corporations negotiate large business deals. For example, the purchasing department, also known as procurement; the marketing team; the legal team; and the financial team could all be involved with the deal in some capacity.

Before you make an external deal, everybody needs to be on the same page. If not, you could, for example, make a deal where you are legally exposed even though it is a financial boon for the company. This is why it's critical to have internal negotiation within the company before you engage in external negotiations.

In this chapter, the "corporation" in question is you. You need to get all of the important parts of yourself on the same page before you have the external negotiation. In this internal negotiation, we'll focus on reconciling the needs and wants of your heart and mind, your emotional self and your rational self.

People often have an implicit understanding that the first negotiation you have to have is within yourself, but what does that really mean? How do you do that? This chapter walks you through what it means, why you should do it, and how you should do it. The Compassionate Curiosity Framework gives you a systematic approach to what seems like, on its surface, a nebulous or ephemeral concept. It gives you a robust approach to confront the intangibles that exist within yourself in order to achieve tangible, external results.

The first, and most important, conflict is inside of us. It's our inner conflict. What makes conflict so difficult is the fact that we focus so much on the external conflict that we don't even recognize the internal conflict at play.

This introspective process is the forgotten part of negotiation preparation. Once you have had this internal negotiation, then you can *properly* prepare for and engage in the external negotiation. This process will help you find clarity and strength.

With this inner conflict we are trying to answer the following questions:

- What do we want?

- Why do we want it?

- Do we have what it takes to get it?

In the Western world, we make the mistake of focusing so much on the process and the outcome that we forget to consider the internal battle, which is just as important as the external battle. What good is it if you go into a conflict and get what you think you want, only to find out that it is not what you really want?

With these difficult conversations, the first person you need to persuade is yourself. If you can't convince yourself, it is going to be incredibly difficult for you to convince others.

Acknowledge Your Emotions

The Compassionate Curiosity Framework can help you to discover the truth about yourself and help uncover the root of your struggles in difficult conversations.

One time, I was working with a client who started a business, but couldn't set boundaries with clients. He said that whenever they pushed him, he would simply agree to whatever terms they wanted. He would let them walk all over him and he couldn't bring himself to say no or push back.

As the conversation continued, we discovered that this was a problem that had plagued him for as long as he could remember. It was a defense mechanism of sorts. Eventually, toward the end of the conversation, we were able to identify the root of the issue.

He was sexually abused by a family friend over the course of two months when in third grade. At first he tried to fight back, but the perpetrator was bigger and stronger and he learned he would incur less damage if he stopped fighting. It was a defense mechanism that he carried into adulthood and into the business world. We decided that it would be best for him to seek professional counseling to address these unresolved issues.

We resumed coaching a few months later and he was a new man. Once he was able to discover the root of the issue, he could find the appropriate solution. Counseling gave him the psychological and emotional balance necessary to perform in these difficult conversations. Discussing the strategies and tactics would have failed to solve the underlying problem.

True strength is found in befriending, respecting, and under- standing the value of the current version of yourself, the past version of yourself, and the version of yourself you want to be. You connect with true self when you are comfortable with every part of yourself. That's when I found my deepest levels of confidence. I have value. I'm worth it. If you believe it, others will believe it, too. Getting to this depth will lead to your authentic self and authenticity is persuasive. But before we can talk about persuasive skills, tactics, and strategies, we need to find your voice. Your voice will be comprised of the person you currently are, the person you want to be, and, whether you like it or not, the person you used to be and don't want to be—the parts of yourself that you reject or find undesirable.

As much as we'd like to, we cannot ignore our emotions. They have value. They provide us with critical information about ourselves, our needs, our wants, our concerns, our fears, and much more. Ignoring them doesn't make them go away. We need to treat emotional discomfort as a signal for further investigation. Ask yourself:

1. What am I feeling?

2. Why am I feeling it?

3. What can I learn from this?

4. Where is the opportunity in this?

5. Where is the threat in this?

Men may find this stage of the process to be particularly difficult because we have been raised to deny our emotions in favor of being stoic and goal-oriented. Men typically prefer to limit themselves to a narrow range of emotions.

Acknowledging emotions is not as easy as it may seem. For example, anger is an emotion that is particularly tricky because in many cases it is not a primary emotion — it is a secondary emotion. This means that anger often comes as a result of another emotion. For men, it is much more socially acceptable to display and embrace anger.

With regard to this stage in the Compassionate Curiosity Framework, this may lead some to abbreviate the analysis of their emotions after they identify the fact that they feel anger. In order to go deeper, ask yourself, "What else am I feeling?" You may find another emotion lurking in the shadows like fear, loneliness, sadness, betrayal, etc.

However, there can be risks with introspection. Sometimes you can do *too much* introspection and end up with a "bug problem." One time I was walking with Kai, who pointed at the ground and said, "What's that?"

I said, "It's a bug, KaiKai." "Why?"

"Because that's how it was made, Kai." "Why?"

"Because its mommy and daddy were bugs." "But why were they bugs?"

"Why were they bugs? I don't know I guess one day they woke up and said, 'Damn, I'm a bug.'"

What's the point? Introspection can become unproductive. Sometimes you won't find anything of value and that's okay. At a certain point, you need to stop asking yourself why and start focusing on what is.

Compassionate Curiosity and Joint Problem-Solving

When using Compassionate Curiosity internally, we need to use the "Five Why Technique" we discussed earlier. We can't simply assume that we understand what we want and why we want it.

If you were a different person tasked with negotiating with yourself, what would you ask yourself? When you get a better understanding of the *why* you'll see the *what* differently as well.

I enjoy gamifying my trainings and coaching sessions as much as possible. One time, I was working with a client who was incredibly intellectual and I felt that her affinity for sterile, rational analysis was getting in the way of her performance. She was in conflict with her business partner who wanted more of the company than she was willing to give.

143

I asked her, "How much equity should your partner have?" She responded by saying, "I offered him 30%."

I said, "You didn't answer my question. Let's play a game called the one second game. I'm going to ask a question and you need to answer within one second. How much equity *should* your business partner have?"

She immediately said, "10-15%." "Why is that?"

"This company was my idea and, although he was doing about 25% of the work with me when we first started, since he moved away he has produced nothing, literally nothing, over the last nine months. At this point he's more of a silent investor than a true partner."

With her first response, instead of telling me what her heart wanted, she tempered the response from her heart with the logic of her head. We were only able to find the truth when she was required to answer those self-directed questions without judging or criticizing herself.

This caused us to adjust our strategy significantly and begin the negotiation with a technique called anchoring where we began the negotiation with a more aggressive opening offer. This resulted in the two parties agreeing to 10% equity.

What would've happened without this emotional investigation? We would've ended up getting a deal where we gave up 30%, which would've been exactly what she asked for, and yet she would've been unsatisfied with the result. We would've been starting the negotiation from a point that would have ultimately been emotionally unacceptable. Then what would've happened? If she got that agreement, she would've been in a long-term relationship filled with resentment she wouldn't be able to explain.

Don't be ashamed of your true desires. You need to start off with some level of emotional honesty with yourself. The thing that makes negotiation and conflict resolution so difficult is the fact that it requires the balance of the seemingly dichotomous forces of reason and emotion. You can't choose one over the other. You need both of them to succeed.

This is where self-compassion comes into play. If you criticize yourself for how you feel or what you want, you will start to feel shame. Shame is antithetical to openness. It will make the process of introspection unnecessarily painful and will result in you failing to investigate your emotions with the requisite amount of depth.

Never let your head accept a deal that your heart rejects. The right financial decision may leave you in a wreck emotionally. The teachings from this book are useless unless you use them to get what you really want.

What is the point of working hard to make a deal that breaks your heart? The right solution will allow you to feel comfortable with the decision you made emotionally. When it's all said and done, you need to feel comfortable on both levels—the rational *and* emotional.

Sometimes we can be too close to the situation and it's difficult to take a broader perspective. If you're struggling to explore your thoughts and feelings yourself, you may benefit from additional assistance. Talking it through with your personal board of directors, comprised of trusted friends, families, or colleagues, would be beneficial. You're essentially outsourcing this internal cognitive exercise. For some of my coaching clients, this process of internal explanation was more valuable than the actual negotiation and conflict management strategies we employed.

Now that you have been armed with a deeper understanding of yourself you can approach the conversation in a much more authentic and powerful way. The sooner we are able to accurately identify and label the emotions that we are feeling the faster we get clarity. The faster we get clarity. The faster we get clarity, the faster we can get emotional relief. When we get emotional relief we are able to perform at a higher level during these difficult conversations.

Chapter 9

EXTERNAL COMPASSIONATE CURIOSITY

"The art of being wise is the art of knowing what to overlook."
William James

The benefit of entering these difficult conversations with a framework is not only that it tells you what you should focus on, but what to ignore. The goal is to simplify these interactions to reduce your fear and anxiety while increasing your confidence. This allows you to marshal your precious cognitive resources and direct them to meaningful dialogue.

The paradox of persuasion is that sometimes speaking less gets you more and being right doesn't mean you will get what you want. You will accomplish more from the questions you ask than the statements you make. "Negotiation is the art of letting them have your way."[63]

The Compassionate Curiosity Framework is rooted in the philosophy that the key to persuasion is to spend more time listening than talking. This takes pressure off of you because your goal is to learn more than teach. It makes the problem of not knowing what to say less of a concern.

What's fascinating about the Compassionate Curiosity Framework is that although you are speaking less, you are exercising more control over the conversation. It gives you a clear strategy and systematic approach to controlling the direction of the conversation, which gives you a greater likelihood of success and productive dialogue. You are exerting quiet control over the process.

When someone knows that they are being sold something or someone is trying to convince them of something, they will naturally put up their defenses. By being inquisitive and asking questions, you are lowering their defenses, which opens them up to subsequent persuasion.

As a father of a two-year-old, I've learned the hard way that you can't put toothpaste back in the tube. Similarly, as a mediator and attorney, I've learned that you can't take back the wrong words once you say them. The best you can do at that point is damage control. Although, the tools in this book *can* help you to fix some of the mistakes you've made, it's critical to understand that the damage can *never be fully repaired*. There will always be scars.

After reading this book, you will be less likely to cause that damage in the first place. It's a lot easier to engage in conflict productively if you avoid the mistakes of saying the wrong thing. Since this approach is focused on asking and listening, it will result in you having less to say, which is good because the less you speak, the less likely you are to say the wrong thing.

The vast majority of the decisions made by humans are made by their emotional mind and then are subsequently rationalized by their logical mind. This is why the Compassionate Curiosity Framework starts with the emotional part of the equation.

The Compassionate Curiosity Framework is fluid. It is not always going to be sequential. In most instances, though it will start with acknowledging emotions, then move to Compassionate Curiosity, and end with joint problem-solving. However, for example, if you're in the problem-solving stage and you encounter an emotional issue, then you can circle back and acknowledge emotions. Similarly, if during the problem-solving stage you recognize a gap in your knowledge, you can revert back to Compassionate Curiosity. The beauty of this framework is that it allows you to know what to do when confronted with specific problems.

Acknowledge Emotions

Earlier this year, I started off every day with hostile negotiations. I take Kai to school in the morning and it was always a battle. My wife is a physician and she goes into the office early and every morning Kai would ask for mommy. I would say, "Kai, mommy is at work. It's time to go to school. Let's brush your teeth." Then he would cry and throw a mini tantrum. This would happen almost every morning.

I knew things were getting bad when he would wake up and immediately start telling me everybody he loved more than me. "I want mommy."

"Mommy is not here. Let's brush your teeth."

"I want grandma."

"Grandma's not here. We need to brush your teeth now."

Then one morning he crossed the line. He said, "I want Uncle Kobie." Now this was hurtful because Kobie is my brother who lives two hours away. Then, to add insult to injury, he said, "I want Buxton." Buxton is my brother's dog. That's when I knew something had to change.

I bought a parenting book that said that the key to persuasion in children is acknowledging emotions.[64] Honestly, as a lawyer, I was offended by the simplicity of the approach. I wanted something more substantive and remarkable. But I was desperate, so I decided to try it.

The next morning Kai woke up and predictably said, "I want mommy."

I said, "It sounds like you love mommy, don't you Kai."

"Yeah."

"Do you miss mommy?"

"Yeah."

"I miss mommy, too. Can you yell 'I love you, mommy!'?"

"I love you, mommy!"

"Are you ready to brush your teeth, Kai?"

"Yeah, let's brush our teeth."

Kai's needs in this scenario where purely emotional. Of course, he did wish his mom was there, but he understood that she was at work and his request wouldn't be granted. However, that hadn't stopped him from asking. Why?

He didn't know how to articulate it, but what he really wanted out of the interaction was my respect and acknowledgment of his current emotional state. He wanted to know that I knew how he felt and that his feelings were legitimate. I didn't need to agree with him, nor did I have to give into his substantive request. He just wanted to be seen.

With the story above, we see that at the beginning of the conversation, I was talking to his amygdala and at the end of the conversation I was talking to his prefrontal cortex. Sometimes people are not in a state where they are even cognitively capable of fully understanding your message. Your most powerful points will fall flat without the engagement of their prefrontal cortex. We are walking them from insanity to sanity, so we can eventually talk to their rational mind.

If children do not feel right emotionally, it will be difficult for them to act right behaviorally. Adults aren't much different. Especially in the business world, we struggle to articulate our emotional needs and wants. As a result, people often make a substantive request in order to fill an emotional gap.

In one of my mediations, a tenant was frustrated with the performance of her landlord and she was suing them for $1,000. She had a litany of complaints and she didn't feel as though they were taking her seriously. She felt disrespected and small.

When I conveyed this to the landlord and shared the story from her perspective, he was shocked. He did not realize that the property manager was performing so poorly. He didn't respond with counterarguments or a counter-proposal. He started by conveying a sincere apology and let her know that he understood why she felt that way and acknowledged that her frustrations were legitimate. He vowed to make sure that the repairs happened in a timely manner.

When she heard that, she unilaterally dropped her lawsuit. She felt heard and satisfied. Once her emotional needs were met, her substantive request disappeared.

These pent-up emotions are like a pressure cooker. Most people use pressure cookers for food, but some bad actors in the past have used pressure cookers as bombs. In acknowledging a negotiating partner's emotions, we allow them to let off steam in a safe, controlled way. We are diffusing a potentially explosive situation and paving the way for productive dialogue.

In order to diffuse someone's emotions, I need to use Compassionate Curiosity to dig deeply into the pain and discomfort they feel. I want them to fully explore the negative emotion so they can get it out of their system.

There's an assumption that the emotions we acknowledge will always have a negative orientation. This isn't the case. Sometimes they feel positively toward themselves and their emotional goal is to get you to see that positivity, too. You see this often with regard to seeing one's value as a person or respecting one's power and authority.

For example, this can be seen in the employee making an unrealistic salary request. They might be replacing their emotional need with a substantive request. Their true goal might be to get you to see that they are a valuable member of the team. They need to know that you know that.

What Do I Say?

Here's a simple three-part structure you can use when acknowledging the emotions of others:

1. State the agreed-upon facts.

2. Demonstrate your appreciation of the impact the situation has on the other party.

3. Make an educated guess as to what they're feeling.

For example, in the landlord tenant mediation I described earlier, I said the following:

1. Your roof was leaking into your child's bedroom, which caused a mold problem.

2. This triggered your child's asthma and gave you a respiratory infection, both of which are serious health concerns.

3. I'm a father, too. I'd imagine the past two months have been incredibly frustrating and scary for you and your family.

Then wait for a response. They will respond by either confirming or clarifying.

She said, "Absolutely! I'm furious! I had to miss work to take care of my daughter and it seems like they don't care."

Then you summarize and reflect your understanding back to them *using the same key words they used*. I said, "I couldn't imagine. You have every right to be *furious*."

Sometimes they might not feel comfortable sharing the depths of their emotions. Don't assume that the fact that they are reluctant to share means that there isn't an emotional barrier. If this happens, you might have to take the first step and tell them how you feel in order to get them to reciprocate. Vulnerability is important in these discussions because it is the social lubricant to that leads to open, effective communication.

Crying in mediation is a regular occurrence. This often embarrasses people and I can tell they are trying to hold back. When- ever this happens, I always say, "It's okay. It would be weird if you weren't crying right now." I say this because I want to normalize the experience. They aren't feeling these emotions because something's wrong with them; they are feeling these emotions because they're a functioning human. I want them to feel safe sharing. The more they share, the more they trust. The more they trust, the more open to influence they become.

How Can We Acknowledge Without Agreement?

Don't mistake empathy and endorsement. Just because we empathize with someone and accept their emotions doesn't mean that we accept or endorse their beliefs or behavior.

We can empathetically set boundaries by acknowledging emotions while alerting them to the limits of their request. Many people make the mistake of doing this while using the word "but." They may say something like, "I understand that you feel frustrated but..." This is problematic because saying "but" negates everything you said previously.

There's a simple solution. Replace the word "but" with the phrase, "the problem is..." Then you fill in the blank with the reason you cannot grant their request. It has the effect of acknowledging emotions while clearly setting boundaries.[65]

Why Is This Important?

Besides the fact that it calms the amygdala, acknowledging these emotions is critical because it creates connection. If we don't take the time to acknowledge emotions or, even worse, we dismiss emotions, we show them we don't care. They may even interpret it as you judging and condemning them for how they feel. Thus, we need to be careful not to reflexively dismiss or contradict what they say with regard to their emotional state.

Compassionate Curiosity

Imagine you've entered a room that's completely dark and your goal is to safely navigate to the other side of the room. What is the first thing you'll want to do? Turn on the light.

This is called the light theory of negotiation. In this metaphor, the darkness represents a lack of knowledge and the light represents information. We turn on the lights by doing research, preparing before the conversation, and asking high-level questions during the conversation. Every time they answer a question, it's like turning on a light switch and illuminating a new part of the room.

A significant portion of our fear and anxiety comes from a lack of information. Since there's not enough light, we can't navigate through the room confidently and we're afraid we'll get hurt. The number one cause of mistakes in these difficult conversations is moving too quickly in a room that's too dark.

The thing is, *you* can't turn on the lights. They need to do it for you. Every time they answer a question, they flip a switch and more light comes on. Your first order of business in a negotiation is to have them turn on the lights so you can move forward confidently. You know your goal might be getting to the other side of the room, but you can't get there if you don't know what obstacles are in your way.

How Do We OperationalizeCompassion?

**The quality of the answer depends on the
quality of the question.**

It's important to avoid over-intellectualizing the term compassion as it relates to the Compassionate Curiosity Framework. Compassion will manifest itself slightly differently in eachperson.

In order to discover what Compassionate Curiosity means to you, take the following steps:

1. Visualize someone you consider to be compassionate. This person can be someone you know or a public figure. Actually close your eyes and see that person.

2. Ask yourself, if this person were in my position, how would they ask questions?

The purpose of this exercise is to help you to moderate your tone as you ask these questions. It also helps you to avoid making the conversation sound like an interrogation.

I've been married for eight years. When I get upset, I become very lawyerly. It's my defense mechanism. My words become precise, academic, strategic, and targeted. Sometimes when I get like this, Whitney accuses me of yelling. I would respond by saying, "Whitney, that's not true. I'm not yelling at you. I don't yell. The definition of yelling requires elevated volume of speech and my volume has not increased." Although I might be "right," I'm not being persuasive and I'm certainly not being likable.

The reality is that she wasn't concerned with the decibel level of my voice; she was offended by my tone. I entered the conversation with an inappropriate mindset. All my communication stemmed from the mindset of an arrogant attorney seeking to prove a point.

One of the most important things I want you to take from this is the fact that there are times where I struggle with this as well. What I should have done was acknowledged the fact that my tone was hurtful instead of being quick to counter. Then I should have compassionately asked her some open-ended questions to get a better understanding of her perspective.

I'll admit that I'm much better at using this tool when I'm at work than I am when I'm at home. This is because as the relationship gets closer, the stakes get higher. There's more to lose and it often inhibits our performance.

Keys to Curiosity

The goal of our curiosity is to gather as much high-quality information as possible. In general, you're trying to uncover the positive they're trying to achieve and the negative they're trying to avoid.[66] The tools at your disposal here are going to be requests for information in the form of open-ended questions and open-ended statements.

Open-ended questions are questions that start with who, what, where, when, how, and why. Of these, it's preferable to stick to what and how questions because questions that start with why are often seen as accusatory.[67] When a toddler does something inexplicable, you typically ask them "Why did you do that?!" Replacing "Why did you do that?!" with "What happened?" or "How did this happen?" is much more productive. It allows you to get the information you want without the risk of triggering feelings of judgment or shame.

Open-ended statements are requests for information that don't end in a question mark but still are meant to solicit a response that requires elaboration.

Examples include:

- Tell me more about...

- Help me to understand...

With regard to sequencing your questions, I favor using the funnel technique. With this technique, you start the conversation by asking broader questions, then you get more specific as the conversation progresses and you get more information.

The goal is to get them to share their key to persuasion. Get them to share what motivates them and the problems they need to be solved. Once they've clearly articulated these things, then you can tailor your arguments to address their core concerns. If you ask the right questions, they will give you the right key.

When I mediate, I prefer to separate the parties so they feel less guarded. I read the case file before the mediation so I know what the plaintiff wants and why they believe they deserve it. Similarly, I've seen the response from the defendant so I know why they disagree with the plaintiff. However, despite this, I start off all of my mediations by saying, "How did we get here?" or "What are you looking to get out of this mediation?" I start the conversation as if I know nothing.

My conversational pattern, in difficult conversations and when I'm building relationships in general, is as follows:

- Ask

- Listen

- Summarize

I will repeat this pattern in some fashion throughout the entire conversation. It's critical to follow the summarization with an *immediate* question as often as possible. This helps to ensure that you're controlling the conversation.

As the host of the Negotiate Anything podcast, my goal is to gather as much information as possible from the guests. Being a podcast host has improved my skills in difficult conversations because I follow the same pattern. The guest ends up talking significantly more than I do, but they're talking about what I want them to talk about because they are being led by my questions.

I start my questions broadly because I want to see the heart be- hind the story, not the pristine version of the story drafted by lawyers with the goal of maximizing persuasion. Another reason why I do this is because it shows me what's truly important to them. For example, I can tell if an issue is important if they repeat certain facts. Then, as the conversation progresses, I start to home in on the most relevant points of the case until we nail down a set of acceptable solutions.

One of the biggest problems people face in these difficult conversations is the feeling of not knowing what to say. If you find yourself in this situation, it's usually a sign that your next move shouldn't be making a statement; it should be asking a question. You don't know what to say because you don't have enough information. Learning more is the solution. You lack the right words because you lack the right information.

There are going to be times when we are tempted to tell people what we want them to know instead of leading them there through questions. We might want to show them the right answer. Instead of telling them how they should think, turn your statement into an open-ended question. This puts you in a position to lead them to your conclusion in a way that makes them feel as though the idea was theirs. Persuasion is more powerful if they feel as though they came to the conclusion themselves.

As you go through this process, the gaps in your knowledge will slowly become filled. When this happens, you may start to run out of questions to ask. Here are some of my go-to questions if I'm not sure what to ask:

- What else do you think I should know?

- What am I missing?

- What other challenges are you facing?

Once I'm satisfied with the information I've received, I'll transition to the joint problem-solving stage by saying something like, "Is there anything else you'd like to address before we move on to discuss solutions?" This puts them on notice that we're entering a new phase of the conversation.

Direct commands encourage direct opposition. In some regards, Compassionate Curiosity is a circuitous route to persuasion. However, this approach increases your likelihood of success because it inspires less resistance.

A hidden benefit is that being genuinely curious forces you to use the prefrontal cortex, the most evolved brain structure on earth. This helps you to avoid amygdala hijacks and allows you to process the vast amount of information you receive at a higher level.

Joint Problem-Solving

Kai's grandma loves doing stereotypically grandmotherly things like making muffins for him. One morning I was trying to be proactive and decided that I would put the muffins in the cupholders in his car seat before I woke him up. I thought it would make the morning more efficient.

When we got downstairs, he asked for muffins and started to pull down the tray from the counter. I said, "No, Kai. Just wait. I have muffins for you already in the car." He didn't like this and he threw a small-scale tantrum. I wasn't too concerned because I thought he'd be excited to see that there were muffins waiting for him in the car. I thought wrong.

When we got to the car I said, "Look, Kai! Muffins!" Kai was unimpressed. He rejected my muffins and crossed his little arms for emphasis.

Kai didn't just want to eat muffins; he wanted to choose them himself. I restricted his autonomy and his feeling of control, so he reclaimed control by rejecting my "reasonable" solution *despite* the fact that accepting my offer was in his best interest.

This is why it's so important to make sure that our counterparts in the process feel as though they played a role in the decision making process. The key is to find creative ways to increase their *perception* of control.

Working Toward Resolution

This is based on the idea of future-focused problem-solving. This approach to collaborative negotiation focuses on what the relationship looks like going forward and what commitments will or will not occur.

I think of this phase as a brainstorming session where both parties share ideas and potential solutions. I structure my proposals in the following way:

1. Given what we know now, I believe that (describe proposal here) would be beneficial for both of us because (explain why it works for you and why it works for them using their own words).

2. What are your thoughts?

Then we listen to hear their perspective and, if necessary, rebuttal. Then we repeat the process. This is the part of the process where you can use persuasive techniques like anchoring and the norm of reciprocity.

I'm resisting the urge to turn this book into a recitation of my favorite persuasive tools. However, I go in-depth with strategies and tactics every week on the Negotiate Anything Podcast if you want to learn more about the tools available during a negotiation.

Sometimes the other side might be lacking in creativity or hesitant to engage in a brainstorming session with you. If that's the case, you can use the "magic question":

If you could wave a magic wand and solve this problem, what would the solution look like? What would need to happen? This helps them to think outside of the box by expanding their view of what's possible.

Encouraging Good Behavior

Throughout the conversation, I want to reinforce good behavior to increase the likelihood that it will continue. I will let them know explicitly that I appreciate the good things that they do.

For example, in my mediations I want people to share information and trust me. Because of that, I say things like the following throughout the conversation:

- "I appreciate your candor."

- "I appreciate you explaining that thoroughly to me."

- "I know that you are in a difficult position right now and I appreciate how you are   handling yourself in this conversation. Most people wouldn't be able to respond in this way."

- "Thank you for that. You're making my job easier."

What I'm doing here is making it clear that their efforts are recognized. I am creating a positive persona for them. I'm implicitly conveying that now I expect them to continue to comport themselves in this way.

People enjoy receiving this recognition and, as a result, they are going to want *more* recognition so they are going to continue to do positive things. Even if a party in the mediation is being particularly mean or nasty, I try to find something to appreciate. Once I'm able to do this, their behavior almost always improves over the course of the mediation.

Compare that to criticizing their behavior, which makes them want to rebel. Even if it does change their behavior, it doesn't improve their mood or their willingness to give you what you want. If you complain and criticize, you shift the power dynamics in your favor in a negative way. People will seek creative ways to reclaim some of that power, and the easiest way for them to do that is for them to ultimately deny you what you want. Remember, you're engaging in this conversation because you need them in some capacity. Otherwise you would've just solved this problem yourself, and they know that. They will wait until they are in a position where they have leverage, and this will come at the most inopportune time: when you are asking for something.

Managing the Inevitable Breakdowns of Communication

You don't need to be good all the time; you just need to be good when it matters.

One of the most interesting things about tennis is the scoring system. In most other sports, the winner is determined based on who had more points overall; in tennis, not all points are created equally. In fact, there are circumstances where a player can lose more total points and still win the match simply because they won the right points. Asking myself, "Did I need that point to win?" helps me to keep my cool in the heat of the moment on the court. I take the same mentality into my difficult conversations.

One time, a tennis commentator said that's the difference between good players and great players. Great players recognize the pressure points in a match and step up when it matters most. You need to understand these pressure points and how to perform when it matters.

We can do a similar analysis in difficult conversations. Not all points are created equally. I may want to win every single point, but the fact of the matter is that I don't need to. You don't need to be perfect all the time; you just need to be good enough when it matters.

Points of Failure

Sometimes in the midst of these conversations, things start to go wrong. You don't know exactly why or how things started to break down; you just know that it's happening and you feel powerless to stop it.

The breakdown of communication is most likely to occur due to an issue in the following three areas:

1. Frame: the storyline you put over the conversation.

2. Pace: how fast or slow you go in the conversation.

3. Direction: the topics of conversation.

Frame

Framing happens early and often in negotiation. It explains the purpose and goal of the conversation. I always seek to frame the conversation positively and in a way that makes me and my position look reasonable. I do this by talking first during the negotiation or connecting via email before the negotiation.

My framing structure looks like this:

1. Appreciation: I appreciate that you took the time to meet with me today to discuss (insert positively framed issue).

2. Clear goal: My goal here is to (insert positively framed goal that can be adopted by the other side). Based on the fact that you're here, I think it's safe to assume that you want the same thing.

3. Positive view of the future: I'm looking forward to working with you on this.

Thus, the storyline of the conversation is that we are two reasonable people with similar goals who will work collaboratively to create a solution. You want to make your frame sound so reasonable and positive that the other side would look ridiculous rejecting it.

It's important to take the initiative and frame first because you don't want to risk the other party putting a negative frame on the conversation. The frame sets the tone for the rest of the interaction. If the frame is combative, the rest of the negotiation is likely to be combative as well.

If you notice the conversation starting to take a negative turn, you can re-frame the conversation to make sure the positive storyline persists.

Pace

My alma mater, The Ohio State Moritz College of Law has the top-ranked dispute resolution program in the country. Earlier this year, I was fortunate enough to be invited to teach the Negotiation and Mediation Advocacy course.

During our mock negotiations, I noticed that the international students almost never get in heated altercations in their negotiations. Even if a classmate was acting aggressively, they seemed to do a better job keeping their cool.

The fact that English was their second language forced them to slow down and process what they said in a deliberate manner. In other words, they had no choice but to engage their prefrontal cortex, which had the result of quieting the amygdala.

Have you noticed that people almost always curse in their native tongue? This happens because cursing is often associated with negative emotions, which originate in the limbic system. These responses are largely instinctual.

Increased pace is often a sign of increased negative emotions, which leads to a decrease in persuasive communication. These conversations can degrade into games of conversational ping pong, where each party is reflexively countering the points of the other.

When we notice this starting to happen, we need to slow things down. Here are three simple techniques to slow down the conversation:

1. Restate the frame: "I just want to take a moment and restate my goal here..."

2. Get curious: "You made a good point there. Can you tell me more about..."

3. Take a break: "Things are moving really fast and it's getting hard for me to keep up. Let's take a quick break and then get back on track."

Direction

These difficult conversations are like road trips. There are multiple *right* ways to get to the desired destination; however, there are even more *wrong* ways that will lead us astray.

As you prepare for these negotiations, it's going to be critical to get a clear understanding of the most important issues to be addressed. This will help you to make sure that you focus the conversation toward issues that matter.

Sometimes the conversation starts to break down because the conversation takes a wrong turn. This often happens when you start discussing irrelevant issues. Irrelevant issues aren't just unhelpful; they are often inflammatory. When we realize that we're getting off track, we need to reorient the conversation to productive topics.

When the conversation starts to go in the wrong direction, I let the person know that I'm still listening to them, then, when I get a chance, I say, "Let's take a step back" in order to slow things down. Then I restate the frame. After I restate the frame, I talk about the key issues by saying, "It seems like we still need to talk about..." I then regain control of the conversation by asking a question that focuses them on a relevant issue by saying, "What are your thoughts on...?"

Compassionate Curiosity in Hostile or Adversarial Negotiations

Last year, I found myself in a heated contract negotiation. My client told me that it was going to be difficult and the guy was living up to his reputation. His fury was on display within the first two minutes. His voice quivered with rage with every word he said.

I felt the emotional rush from my amygdala and it told me I could fight back, run, or sit there and take it. But I remembered there's another option—I could use Compassionate Curiosity.

I recognized that *he* was experiencing an amygdala hijack. So I gathered myself and started by acknowledging his emotions and finding something to appreciate. I said, "First of all, I want to thank you for sharing. I didn't recognize the impact this situation had on you before this call. I can tell this is incredibly frustrating for you."

I spent the first 20 minutes of the conversation listening to his emotional rant. I made sure to show him I was listening by regularly summarizing and acknowledging his emotion.

As he started to calm down, I started to shift my questions away from his emotions toward more substantive issues.

I asked...

- What are your main concerns?

- How can we help?

- What would work for you?

As he answered these questions, he started to calm down. In less than an hour, he gave my client exactly what we were looking for. By the end of the call, we were laughing and joking with each other.

Resistance and difficulty are inevitable parts of the process. A hostile approach doesn't require a hostile response. You can still use the Compassionate Curiosity Framework as long as you stay keenly aware of your needs and limits.

Many people have internalized the belief that you can either use a win-win or win-lose approach in negotiation. This is a false dichotomy. Negotiation styles fall on a spectrum between more cooperative negotiators and more competitive negotiators. We have a natural point on this spectrum where we will live due to our personal dispositions; however, the best negotiators will be the ones who can slide on that spectrum depending on the situation. If you are a hammer, everything will look like a nail. Notice that the best builders have more than a hammer in their toolbox.

As a business lawyer, I negotiate with opposing counsel and I often teach attorneys and people who are in the position of buying and selling on behalf of large corporations. The Compassionate Curiosity Framework is still the foundation of my negotiations and my trainings.

My negotiation strategy could be called cautiously cooperative. With this approach, you start off being cooperative, but you are open to the possibility you could get information that lets you know that you shouldn't trust this person or be as generous because they will take advantage of you. If you are generous and they don't reciprocate, then the best thing for you to do is protect yourself. You should always comport yourself with honor and dignity, but that doesn't mean you need to be naïve.

When you are in adversarial situations, like litigation, you need to spend significantly more time preparing and strategizing before the conversation. You will also spend less time acknowledging emotions and significantly more time getting curious and swapping solutions. However, the key difference in these adversarial negotiations is to engage in the process with more of a focus on maximizing value, claiming value, and protecting your interests. In this situation, it would be best to couple the Compassionate Curiosity Framework with other tested tools of persuasion to put yourself in the best position to maximize your substantive outcomes.

In your preparation, you especially want to pay attention to the precise words you will use to clearly establish your boundaries. For example, if they request something that is incompatible with your needs, you can respectfully reject their offer by using the "no sandwich."

There are three steps to the no sandwich:

1. State your yes—This is where you clearly articulate the *positive reason* that lies behind your no. There is a yes behind every no. You're letting them know what is causing you to say no.

2. State you no—This is where you succinctly and clearly reject their substantive request.

3. State your yes to the relationship—This is where you let the other side know that your "no" was limited to that specific request and you still want to continue the negotiation and the relationship.[68]

Here's an example: if I'm negotiating with another attorney and they offer something that doesn't meet the needs of my clients, I might say something like this:

1. Based on the financial goals of my client and the other options on the table, it won't be in our best interest to accept that offer.

2. Because of that, I have to say no to that option.

3. However, we're here to negotiate and I still think there's a way we can make this work.

Then I'll continue the conversation by implementing the Compassionate Curiosity Framework and using more advanced negotiation techniques to put myself in the best position to get the best deal for my client. The remainder of the negotiation will be a combination of the following tools:

1. Compassionate Curiosity—Utilizing the Compassionate Curiosity Framework to create connection, learn more about the situation, and swap solutions.

2. No Sandwich—Clearly setting boundaries.

3. Higher Level Techniques—Using higher-level persuasive tactics to try to create and claim as much value as possible.

But What If I'm Evil?

What if you don't care about creating strong relationships or treating people with respect? Should you still use the Compassionate Curiosity Framework?

You should use Compassionate Curiosity because it puts you in the best position to get what you want. It puts you in the best psychological state to perform at a high level and walks the other person from a potentially detrimental emotional response to a position where they can engage in rational decision-making. It accomplishes all of that while providing you with a simple way to defend yourself even in the most hostile of negotiations.

Common Questions and Concerns

With all of these common questions, the Compassionate Curiosity Framework serves as a solution. However, there are going to be additional strategies for specific points within the framework that will differs lightly from topic to topic.

Negotiating While Young

A lot of my listeners are educated young professionals who find themselves in positions of leadership soon after graduation. This often comes with the awkward realization that they have been tasked with managing people with decades more experience than they have. This often comes with a feeling of resentment from the older subordinates, which makes it difficult for the young professionals to lead. They have the position and status, but it seems as though they can't get the respect. Thus, they often ask, "How do I negotiate with somebody who has significantly more experience than I do?"

The people with more experience feel as though they have earned a certain level of respect and admiration. As such, they will be reluctant to feel in any way   subordinate or inferior to a newer, younger colleague. Furthermore, they will likely be completely unwilling to admit that they were persuaded or out-negotiated by a younger professional. However, they will be willing to say that they helped you out.

People feel more comfortable giving help than receiving help. Receiving help means you need to admit some kind of weak- ness and admit that, to a certain extent, you can't do it by yourself. The person giving help, however, feels empowered and capable. We help people because it makes us feel powerful. It makes us feel good about ourselves.

Younger professionals can leverage this by shifting their approach to the conversation from giving demands or orders to soliciting help. For example:

1. Acknowledge emotion: I know you've been here for 20 years, so you know this organization better than almost anyone.

2. Compassionate curiosity: We've been experiencing (state agreed-upon facts). Given your experience, I want your help to figure this out. What are our biggest challenges?

3. Joint problem-solving: I think (insert solution here) could work. What do you think?

This minor tweak in the approach will give them the emotional payment they are looking for and increase their likelihood to comply. They will feel more respected and, as a result, they are more likely to give you what you want.

Limited Time

What if you don't have time to have a quality conversation and go through all the steps with the depth and care that you would like?

Utilizing the Compassionate Curiosity Framework can take time, and the amount of time varies based on the emotional and substantive barriers in front of each party. The reality is, sometimes you simply don't have enough time to execute the strategy as thoroughly as you would like. Sometimes you don't have time to go through the introspection that comes with internal Compassion Curiosity. Sometimes you don't have the time to have the conversation go through all of the three stages thoroughly. However, this doesn't mean that you abandon the strategy; it means that you modify it.

One of the most important things that should be discussed is the expectation each party has about the interaction. If one party wants to talk for a longer period of time than another party and that is not addressed early, it could cause serious problems and impede your ability to reach agreement.

Be transparent and let them know that you don't have the time and explain why you don't have the time. You are managing their expectations so when you seem hurried, frantic, or impatient, they will give you some grace and be more willing to accept that reality because you let them know beforehand.

What you might end up doing before the discussion is deciding whether or not it would be better to break this conversation into parts. Maybe this is the beginning of the conversation and you finish it at another time. However, if that is not feasible, you have no choice but to use an accelerated path. As you move from step to step, take a brief moment to reframe the discussion. Constantly remind the person that the only reason you are pushing the conversation forward in a somewhat unnatural fashion is because of the time constraint. You want to remind them that the rush isn't necessarily coming from you personally; it's coming from outside forces. This makes it less likely for them to identify any negativity with you because of the time issue.

Chapter 10

COMPASSIONATE CURIOSITY VS. BIAS

The Compassionate Curiosity Framework is a powerful tool as it relates to bias. We can use it to address our internal battle against bias as well as the external one.

What is Implicit Bias?

I started working with a stylist before my TEDx Talk, Finding Confidence in Conflict. One of the things he said was that given my complexion, I would look good in pastels. He suggested that I start wearing more lavender, pink, and yellow. This evoked a shockingly forceful response from me.

"No. No. No. No. I love lavender. I love pink. But I never, ever wear yellow."

This response caught me off guard. Why did I say that? What do I have against yellow?

I went home and realized that I didn't have any yellow clothing in my closet. Then I thought back and realized that I hadn't worn any yellow in over 10 years. However, I remembered that in grade school and high school, I used to wear yellow all the time. What happened?

Then it hit me. I am a proud graduate of THE Ohio State University. Our school colors are scarlet and gray and the school colors of our arch rival, Michigan, are maize (yellow) and blue. As a freshman, wearing yellow could result in anything from playful ridicule to forceful reproach. I learned quickly that yellow was an unacceptable color for a wardrobe and I changed my style appropriately.

This is an example of an implicit (unconscious) bias. A bias is a preference toward or bias against something.[69] These biases are natural, though dangerous, byproducts of the human mind's affinity toward mental shortcuts and categorization.[70] Our biases are informed by our family, friends, religious beliefs, political beliefs, the media we consume, and much more. These preferences will develop as we are consistently exposed to these messages throughout our lives.

It's important to be aware of the biases that exist inside of ourselves and inside of others because they pose a significant threat to our ability to connect and persuade. More specifically, implicit biases are problematic because:

1. They result in us giving preferential treatment and deference to certain groups of people while treating other groups with skepticism and disrespect, which leads to unfair and inappropriate outcomes.

2. They impede our ability to connect with others and build trust, which negatively impacts the free flow of information.

3. They could have a negative impact on how others treat us.

It's critical for us to analyze the biases that might be at play within every social interaction because none of us is immune to bias. Having bias isn't something to be ashamed of; however, having bias and not doing anything about it, is.

Dealing with Bias in Ourselves

The Compassionate Curiosity Framework, when used internally, provides you with a tool that you can use to address your own implicit biases.

First, you need to acknowledge the biases that could be at play within the conversation, either for you or your conversational counterpart. Implicit biases are usually not something you are consciously aware of, so taking the time to evaluate your actions and instinctive attitudes is important.

Second, you need to get curious about the origins of your biases and investigate how they impact the way you navigate these conversations. It's important to engage in this process with compassion so you don't vilify yourself. Self-vilification leads to shame and shame leads to withdrawal.

Lastly, you need to prepare by creating strategies to break through the biases **before** you address the substantive issues at play in the conversation. Once you've completed this process of preparation, you will be ready to engage in the conversation.

Think of it as the conflict before the conflict. If you fail to recognize the first conflict, you will struggle in the second conflict. This small tweak can work wonders when it comes to having difficult conversations with people with different backgrounds.

Minority groups don't get a pass. An important, but often overlooked, point is that people who have some kind of minority status can make the mistake of focusing solely on the biases that are against them without addressing the biases they harbor within themselves. Often, due to years of mistreatment, members of minority groups develop biases against the majority. These biases make it difficult for the members of the minority group to connect with people in the majority and, as a result, their biases create a self-fulfilling prophecy where their fears of what might happen in the interaction come to pass in large part *because of those fears,* not in spite of them.

Breaking Through Bias in Others

After you do an analysis of the biases that exist inside of you, you need to consider what biases could possibly exist in others that could serve as a barrier to achieving your goals in the difficult conversation. It's important to understand the biases that people likely have against you. Once you understand those biases, you get a better understanding of the undercurrent in the negotiation that lies before you.

I was a psychology tutor in undergrad. One of the students I tutored was from South Korea. We lived close to each other, so we would walk back to the dorms together after our sessions and chat. One time, we ran into one of my friends. We greeted each other and we had our normal pleasantries. I mentioned that we were just leaving a tutoring session. He said, "Oh, what's he tutoring you in?" And this was *my friend*. He didn't know my friend from Korea at all, but he assumed that the Asian student was tutoring the black student, not the other way around.

This experience and several like it made me realize that one of the biases against black males is an assumption of inferior intelligence. I now know this is a hidden barrier for me as I negotiate.

Another bias black males face is the fear of aggression. One time my friend (another black male) and I were leaving the gym at night. There was a white couple walking towards us on the same side of street. They were so in love that they didn't see us until we were about ten yards away. The man looked up and saw two black men laughing and talking to each other wearing hoodies walking in his direction. He responded by violently pulling his girlfriend's arm and dragging her across to the other side of the street to "safety." The response was so reflexive and so forceful that my immediate concern was for the young woman's shoulder. That's when I recognized that people see me differently.

Negotiating around implicit bias must also be implicit, not explicit. I can't say, "I'm black so most likely you think I'm stupid and scary. But I assure you that I'm not." It needs to be subtle.

If you are dealing with implicit bias, there is a high likelihood that the person on the other side hasn't gone through the introspective process to discover whether or not they harbor these biases. This means that if you were to address the issue explicitly, they would deny that bias exists in them. That potential conversation would be unproductive at best and highly offensive at worst.

This is another example of where giving the benefit of the doubt is beneficial. Implicit bias is by definition a subconscious mechanism. They most likely are not harboring these biases with malicious intent.

Remember, the goal here is cohesion and persuasion. If addressing bias isn't the specific topic of conversation, then you would be better served to avoid direct discussion of the issue. Remember, our goal is at all times to put ourselves in the best position for success.

I break through biases by subtly communicating three points early on in the interaction: I am intelligent, I am not a threat, and I am like the person on the other side.

Intelligence

The way that I choose to address the potential negative bias regarding intelligence is through dress, title, and grammar. When I know I'm having a serious discussion in the business world, I choose to dress well because there is an assumption of intelligence and credibility that comes with formal wear. This is especially important to me as an attorney.

In an interesting study on jaywalking, researchers discovered that groups of people were more likely to jaywalk if somebody who is dressed professionally jaywalks first. If the person is not dressed professionally, the people around them are less likely to follow their lead.[71]

Your outward appearance speaks volumes before you even open your mouth. I want to create an assumption of authority and credibility before the conversation begins in order to counteract the negative implicit assumption that could serve as a barrier to persuasion.

Finding ways to alert people to my education is equally as important. I do this by including the letters I've earned after my email signature and on business cards—Kwame Christian, Esq., M.A. Similarly, when I start talking to people in business contexts, I am more formal. Then, as the conversation progresses and the relationship begins to form, I start to relax my approach.

Not a Threat

I was giving a conflict management and leadership seminar for community leaders last month. One young black male said that people often assume that he is getting aggressive or is intentionally trying to intimidate them when he gets passionate about an issue. He then asked what he could do to address this.

I posed this question to the audience, "If a lion could speak, could we understand him? Why or why not?"[72] This is an interesting thought experiment to encourage discussion. The audience came to the conclusion that we wouldn't be able to fully understand him due in large part to the following reasons:

1. The lion has a completely different lived experience. It would be difficult for us to relate because our backgrounds are so different.

2. We are used to seeing the lion as the king of the jungle and at the top of the food chain. As a result, it's difficult for us to see the lion as anything other than an apex predator. Therefore, no matter what the lion says or how it says it, we will still see its words and actions as threatening.

Then I looked at him and said, "I'm sorry but you look like a lion to me, brother. I've noticed that I'm a lion, too. The question is, what can we do about it?"

I know that being a larger black male can result in people feeling physically intimidated around me. Over the course of my lifetime, I've recognized in many situations if I want to connect with people, then I have to take the first step to make them feel comfortable. I act as though subconsciously the people are asking themselves, "Is this man a threat to me?" I've adjusted my body language to try to answer that question for them early on in the relationship. This leads me to smile more and be friendlier. If we think of it in terms of a relationship bank account, I assume that I am starting off with a negative balance and *before the relationship even begins,* I need to make a deposit of niceness to bring the balance to zero.

As always, my goal in these interactions is to put myself in the best position possible to be persuasive, get what I want, and make investments into the relationship bank account. Staying keenly aware of the biases that may impede my progress is an important part of that.

An important caveat is that this must be done in a way that is still part of your authentic self because authenticity is persuasive. If you feel like behaving in this manner compromises who you are, then don't do it. Remember, we can use the Compassionate Curiosity Framework internally in order to determine whether or not our heart and mind are aligned as we navigate these difficult conversations.

I'm Like You

Lastly, a recent study on implicit bias discovered that you can reduce the negative impact of implicit bias by demonstrating that you and the other person are part of the same in-group.[73] If someone sees you as being part of the same tribe, then they will look more favorably upon you.

This is something that has been well-documented in psychological literature for decades. However, it's only recently that it was clinically demonstrated to serve as a way that you can counterbalance the negative biases that are against you. Because of this finding, I dedicate a portion of my pre-negotiation preparation to finding opportunities for connection through similarities.

Here are the top five most likely places for similarities:

1. Schooling

2. Geographical similarities

3. Parenting

4. Sports affiliations and hobbies

5. Professional background

I would usually share the similarity early on in the interaction either in the email leading up to the conversation or "happen to mention it" early on in the conversation. For example, I might end an email with PS—it is nice to see another fellow Buckeye doing well in this industry! This is what I would use if the person on the other side is a fellow graduate of The Ohio State University. Or early on in the conversation I might talk about something I did with my son recently. This is something I would say if I know that the person is a parent as well.

These subtle tweaks in my approach have paid big dividends. They've made it easier for me to connect and persuade as I navigate the business world.

Conclusion

Bias has a different impact on different people, depending on where they are situated in society. Therefore, bias affects me differently than it might affect the white man and white woman and Asian man and Asian woman, etc. Regardless, the first step is to identify likely biases that exist. We need to build rapport with those biases in mind. So when I'm building rapport with somebody of a different race who doesn't know me at all, I understand that one of the first things I can do to make them feel comfortable.

CONCLUSION

If you've read this far there is something about this message that resonates with you. What's your goal? What would your life look like if you improved your ability to perform in these difficult conversations? How would that change the way you see yourself? How would that change the way others see you? Regardless of your motivations, reading this book is a powerful step in achieving those goals.

Remember, the goal is continuous improvement, not perfection. In many cases, the determination of progress is going to be largely subjective. A good way to determine the status of your progress is by asking the following questions:

1. Am I putting myself in the best position for success?

2. Are my skills improving?

3. Are my outcomes improving?

4. Are my relationships improving?

Although we are faced with difficult conversations on a daily basis, few people ever have the opportunity to learn about and practice this skill. When I put on negotiation and conflict management seminars, I always ask the same question. How many of you have ever taken a course on negotiation or conflict management? It's never more than 5% of the individuals who have had that kind of training.

This oversight creates opportunity. The ability to handle these difficult conversations may be one of the single greatest skills distinguishing the successful from the unsuccessful.

We have bad role models today with regard to difficult conversations. The model we always see is the reality TV show/ news media style of confrontation, which involves yelling, not listening, and attempting to embarrass, humiliate, or shame the other side. When we see that, we often make the mistake of mimicking those behaviors.

These kinds of conversations don't bring us together; they can only push us apart. The problem is that when we invite this style of communication into our lives, we end up hurting relationships and not getting what we want. We're not being persuasive and we're not working toward a tangible outcome of changed hearts and minds.

We are living in a time where it is getting harder and harder to have difficult conversations. It seems as though people are struggling more to connect and peacefully resolve their issues. Things have gotten so combative that people are unwilling to engage at all. The rhetoric in our political climate is more vitriolic and divisive than ever. Unfortunately, some of the same tendencies leak into the business world.

The consistent implementation of the Compassionate Curiosity Framework not only puts you in the best position to get what you need out of these difficult conversations, but it also positions you to be on the forefront of this new wave of positive communication. It is our responsibility to speak up and say something if we really care about the relationship and making positive change.

Your willingness to change is the first step in what could be a massive ripple effect that reverberates around your personal ecosystem. The way you comport yourself in these difficult conversations will rub off on the people around you. Your friends, family, and colleagues will see the change in you and follow your lead.

My approach to difficult conversations has lead to positive changes in the way that the people around me now interact with one another. As a mediator, I've seen how my use of Compassionate Curiosity slowly starts to change the affect and behavior of the participants as the mediation progresses. Don't underestimate your impact.

Remember, your ability to perform in difficult conversations is a skill, not a talent. You can improve. However, it's important to realize that the Compassionate Curiosity Framework is not a panacea for the psychological and emotional barriers you face. Improvement isn't going to happen overnight. It's going to be hard and you're going to make mistakes. But we don't have these difficult conversations because they are easy, we have them because it's worth it.

WAIT! MORE RESOURCES

This book gives you a great foundation for having these difficult conversations but there's much more to learn and we can help you every step of the way.

Online Course: Negotiate Anything: Finding Confidence in Conflict.

Visit our website: Gain access to our robust online program that will give you the confidence you need to succeed and the most powerful persuasive techniques. Visit www.AmericanNegotiationInstitute.com/Course and use the word "**confidence**" for a 10% discount.

Custom Workshops and Training: We work with organizations just like yours to create custom trainings. Visit our website to see how we can help.

Coaching: We also provide 1 on 1 coaching for professionals looking to get an edge or overcome their personal barriers for success.

Negotiate Anything Podcast: This is the #1 negotiation podcast in the world. We have leading experts on the show every week to share their best tips.

Ask With Confidence Podcast: This podcast is all about women in negotiation. Our host, Katherine Knapke, has incredible women leaders on the show to explore how to be successful in negotiation.

MEET KWAME

Bestselling author and speaker Kwame Christian is the Director of the American Negotiation Institute and a subject matter expert in the field of negotiation and conflict resolution. Kwame has conducted workshops throughout North America and abroad, and is a highly sought after national keynote speaker.

The host of the world's most popular negotiation podcast, Negotiate Anything, Kwame is dedicated to empowering others through the art and science of negotiation and persuasion. The show features leading experts in the field to deliver the best-in-class content. Now downloaded more than 1,500,000 times, Negotiate Anything has a dedicated and growing following with listeners in more than 180 countries around the world.

Kwame's TEDx Dayton talk, Finding Confidence in Conflict, was the most popular TEDx Talk on the topic of conflict in 2017, and has been viewed over 140,000 times. His book, *Finding Confidence in Conflict: How to Negotiate Anything and Live Your Best Life* (formerly entitled *Nobody Will Play With Me*) and has helped countless individuals overcome the fear, anxiety, and emotion often associated with difficult conversations through a branded framework called Compassionate Curiosity.

As an attorney and mediator with a Bachelors of Arts in Psychology, a Master of Public Policy, and a Juris Doctorate (Law Degree), Kwame brings a unique multidisciplinary approach to making difficult conversations easier. He also serves as an adjunct professor for Otterbein University's

MBA program, as well as The Ohio State University's Moritz College of Law in the top-ranked dispute resolution program in the country.

Notes

[1] Society of Clinical Psychology. *What Is Cognitive Behavioral Therapy?* American Psychological Association

[2] Society of Clinical Psychology. *What Is Cognitive Behavioral Therapy?* American Psychological Association

[3] Complicated. (2010). In *Dictionary.com*. Retrieved from https://www.-dictionary.com/browse/complicated

[4] Complex. (2010). In dictionary.com. Retrieved from https://www.dictionary.com/browse/complex

[5] Kahneman, D. (2011). *Thinking, Fast and Slow*. New York, NY: Farrar, Straus and Giroux.

[6] Diamond, A. (2014). Want to Optimize Executive Functions and Academic Outcomes?: Simple, Just Nourish the Human Spirit. *Minnesota Symposia on Child Psychology*, *37*, 205–232.

[7] *Understanding The Stress Response*. (n.d.). Retrieved from https://www.health.harvard.edu/staying-healthy/understanding-the-stress-response.

[8] Arnsten, A. F. T. (2009). Stress signaling pathways that impair prefrontal cortex structure and function. *Nature Reviews. Neuroscience, 10*(6), 410–422. http://doi.org/10.1038/nrn2648

[9] Johnson, S. B., Blum, R. W., & Giedd, J. N. (2009). Adolescent maturity and the brain: the promise and pitfalls of neuroscience research in adolescent health policy. *The Journal of adolescent health : official publication of the Society for Adolescent Medicine, 45*(3), 216-21.

[10] Doidge, N. (2015). *The Brain's Way of Healing: Remarkable Discoveries and Recoveries from the Frontiers of Neuroplasticity*.

[11] Brown, B. (2016). *Daring Greatly: How the Courage to be Vulnerable Transforms the Way We Live, Love, Parent, and Lead*. London: Penguin Books.

[12] Christian, K., & Lev, P. (2018, May 7). How to Negotiate with Confidence as an Entrepreneur [Audio blog post]. Retrieved October 4, 2018, from https://americannegotiationinstitute.com/most-recent-epi-sodes/

[13] King, Martin Luther. "Letter from a Birmingham Jail." 16 April 1963.

[14] Nance, V. (n.d.). Creator of Anarchy Waffles [Interview]

[15] McKay, Matthew, and Patrick Fanning. *Self-Esteem: A Proven Program of Cognitive Techniques for Assessing, Improving, and Maintaining Your Self-Esteem*. New Harbinger, 2016

[16] Miller, Anna Medaris. "The Science of Awkwardness." *U.S. News & World Report*, 23 Nov. 2015, health.usnews.com/health-news/ health-wellness/articles/2015/11/23/the-science-of-awkwardness.

[17] Shepardson, David. "2017 Safest Year on Record for Commercial Passenger Air Travel: Groups." *Reuters*, Thomson Reuters, 1 Jan. 2018, www.reuters.com/article/us-aviation-safety/2017-safest-year-on-record- for-commercial-passenger-air-travel-groups-idUSKBN1EQ17L.

[18] "Vital Signs." *Centers for Disease Control and Prevention*, 18 July 2016, www.cdc.gov/vitalsigns/motor-vehicle-safety/index.html.

[19] Watts, D. J. (2011). *Everything is Obvious*: *Once You Know the Answer*. Crown Business.

[20] Chansky, Tamar. *Freeing Yourself From Anxiety: 4 Simple Steps to Overcome Worry and Create the Life You Want*. 2012.

[21] *Anxiety*, American Psychological Association, www.apa.org/top- ics/anxiety/.

[22] Frankl, Viktor E., and J. *Man's Search for Meaning*. Beacon Press, 2017.

[23] Chansky, Tamar. *Freeing Yourself from Anxiety: 4 Simple Steps to Overcome Worry and Create the Life You Want*. Da Capo Press, 2012.

[24] Chansky, Tamar. *Freeing Yourself from Anxiety: 4 Simple Steps to Overcome Worry and Create the Life You Want*. Da Capo Press, 2012.

[25] Chansky, Tamar. *Freeing Yourself from Anxiety: 4 Simple Steps to Overcome Worry and Create the Life You Want*. Da Capo Press, 2012.

[26] Chansky, Tamar. *Freeing Yourself from Anxiety: 4 Simple Steps to Overcome Worry and Create the Life You Want*. Da Capo Press, 2012.

[27] Shaw, G. B., & Holroyd, M. (1988). An Unsocial Socialist: A Novel. London: Virago.

[28] Mindset. (2010). In *Dictionary.com*. Retrieved from https:// www.dictionary.com/browse/mindset.

[29] Kaufman, C., Psy.D. (2012). Carolyn Kaufman Psy.D. Psychology for Writers Using Self-Fulfilling Prophecies to Your Advantage [Abstract]. *Psychology Today*. Retrieved from https://www.psychologyto- day.com/ us/blog/psychology-writers/201210/using-self-fulfilling-prophe-cies-your-advantage.

[30] Ariely, D. (2011). The Upside of Irrationality: The Unexpected *Benefits of Defying Logic*. Harper.

[31] Howe, M. L., & Knott, L. M. (2015). The fallibility of memory in judicial processes: lessons from the past and their modern consequences. *Memory (Hove, England)*, *23*(5), 633-56.

[32] Dobrin, A. (n.d.). Your Memory Isn't What You Think It Is. Retrieved from https://www.psychologytoday.com/us/blog/am-i- right/ 201307/your-memory-isnt-what-you-think-it-is

[33] Ariely, D. (2011). The Upside of Irrationality: The Unexpected *Benefits of Defying Logic*. Harper

[34] Symptom. (2010). In *Dictionary.com*. Retrieved from https:// www.dictionary.com/browse/symptom.

[35] Frankl, Viktor E., and J. *Man's Search for Meaning*. Beacon Press, 2017.

[36] California Department of Parks and Recreation. (n.d.). About Coast Redwoods. Retrieved from https://www.parks.ca.gov/?page_ id=22257

[37] Pandolfini, B. (n.d.). *Every Move Must Have a Purpose: Strategies from Chess for Business and Life*. New York: Hyperion.

[38] www.americannegotiationinstitute.com/workbook

[39] [Charisma on Command]. (2018, September 24). *How to Com- mand Respect Without Being a Jerk* [Video File]. Retrieved from https:// www.youtube.com/watch?v=GFphNr0FK-0

[40] Speaker, Waldinger. Robert. Nov. 2015. What Makes a Good Life? Lessons from the Longest Study on Happiness [Video file]. Retrieved from https://www.ted.com/talks/robert_waldinger_what_makes_a_good_ life_lessons_from_the_longest_study_on_happiness?language=en

[41] Nance, V. (n.d.). Creator of Anarchy Waffles [Interview]

[42] Lie. (2010). In *Dictionary.com*. Retrieved from https://www.dictionary.com/browse/lie.

[43] Lie. (2010). In *Dictionary.com*. Retrieved from https://www.dictionary.com/browse/lie.

[44] Feminism, the belief in social, economic, and political equality of the sexes.

[45] Babcock, L., & Laschever, S. (2007). *Women Don't Ask: The High Cost of Avoiding Negotiation--and Positive Strategies for Change*. Bantam.

[46] Shell, G. R. (2006). *Bargaining for Advantage: Negotiation Strategies for Reasonable People*.

[47] Babcock, L., & Laschever, S. (2007). *Women Don't Ask: The High Cost of Avoiding Negotiation--and Positive Strategies for Change*. Bantam.

[48] Confidence. In *Oxforddictionaries.com*. Retrieved from https:// en.oxforddictionaries.com/definition/confidence.

[49] Confidence. In *Oxforddictionaries.com*. Retrieved from https:// en.oxforddictionaries.com/definition/confidence.

[50] Kay, K., & Shipman, C. (2018). *The Confidence Code: The Science and Art of Self-Assurance--What Women Should Know*. New York, NY: Harper-Business, an imprint of HarperCollins.

[51] Navarro, J., & Karlins, M. (2015). What Every BODY is Saying: An Ex-FBI Agent's Guide to Speed-Reading People. New York, NY: Harper Collins

[52] Babcock, L., & Laschever, S. (2007). *Women Don't Ask: The High Cost of Avoiding Negotiation--and Positive Strategies for Change*. Bantam.

[53] Kay, K., & Shipman, C. (2018). *The Confidence Code: The Science and Art of Self-Assurance--What Women Should Know*. New York, NY: Harper-Business, an imprint of HarperCollins.

[54] Kay, K., & Shipman, C. (2018). *The Confidence Code: The Science and Art of Self-Assurance--What Women Should Know*. New York, NY: Harper-Business, an imprint of HarperCollin

55 Purdue University. (2012, April 3). Golfers can improve their putt with a different look: Visualize a great big hole. *Science Daily*. Retrieved October 20, 2018 from www.sciencedaily.com/releas- es/2012/04/120403140036.htm.

56 Cialdini, R. B. (2006). *Influence: The Psychology of Persuasion*. Harper Business.

57 Lunt, P. (2009). Stanley Milgram: Understanding Obedience and Its Applications. Basingstoke, Hampshire: Palgrave Macmillan.

58 Kay, K., & Shipman, C. (2018). *The Confidence Code: The Science and Art of Self-Assurance--What Women Should Know*. New York, NY: Harper-Business, an imprint of HarperCollins.

59 Jiang, J. (n.d.). Retrieved October 28, 2018, from https://www. ted.-com/talks/jia_jiang_what_i_learned_from_100_days_of_rejection

60 Don E. Davis, PhD, an assistant professor of counseling and psycholog- ical services at Georgia State University [*Journal of Counseling Psycholo- gy*, 2015].

61 Neff, K., & Germer, C. (n.d.). *The Mindful Self-Compassion Workbook*.

62 Moran, B. P., & Lennington, M. (2013). *The 12 Week Year: Get More Done in 12 weeks Than Others Do in 12 Months*. Hoboken, NJ: Wiley.

63 Lax, D., & Sebenius, J. (2006). 3-D Negotiation. Harvard Business Review. Retrieved from https://hbr.org/ideacast/2006/11/harvard-business-ideacast-15-3.html.

64 Farber, A., & Mazlish, E. (n.d.). *How to Talk So Kids Will Listen & Listen So Kids Will Talk*.

65 Farber, A., & Mazlish, E. (n.d.). *How to Talk So Kids Will Listen & Listen So Kids Will Talk*.

66 Beulow, Beth & Cravener, Veronica. How Can I Say This....[Audio podcast]. Retrieved from http://theintrovertentrepreneur.com/category/podcast/.

67 Voss, C., & Raz, T. (2017). *Never Split the Difference: Negotiating as if Your Life Depended on it*. Place of publication not identified: Harper Business.

[68] Ury, W. (2008). *The Power of a Positive No: How to Say No and Still Get to Yes.* New York: Bantam Books.

[69] Bias. (2010). In *Dictionary.com.* Retrieved from https://www.dictionary.com/browse/bias.

[70] Understanding Implicit Bias. (n.d.). Retrieved from http://kirw- aninstitute.osu.edu/research/understanding-implicit-bias/

[71] Mullen, B., Copper, C., & Driskell, J. E. (1990). Jaywalking as a Function of Model Behavior. Personality and Social Psychology Bulletin, 16(2), 320-330. doi:10.1177/0146167290162012

[72] Wittgenstein, L. (2009). Philosophical investigations. Chichester: Wiley-Blackwell.

[73] Scroggins, W. A., Mackie, D. M., Allen, T. J., & Sherman, J. W. (2015). Reducing Prejudice With Labels. Personality and Social Psychology Bulletin, 42(2), 219-229. doi:10.1177/0146167215621048

.

Made in the USA
Monee, IL
11 August 2020

38008215R00115